To John & Gill,

From Janet & Sally
Lot et Garonne
July 2003?

Seek and Sink

Bracknell Paper No. 2
A Symposium on the Battle of the Atlantic

21 October 1991

Sponsored jointly by the Royal Air Force Historical Society and the
Royal Air Force Staff College Bracknell

Copyright © 1992 by Royal Air Force Historical Society

First published in the UK in 1992

ISBN 0 9519824 0 0

All rights reserved. No part of this book may be reproduced or transmitted in any form or by any means, electronic or mechanical including photocopying, recording or by any information storage and retrieval system, without permission from the Publisher in writing.

Printed by FotoDirect Ltd., Brighton

Royal Air Force Historical Society

Contents

Preface
Quotation
1. Opening Remarks: Air Vice-Marshal R. G. Peters
2. Chairman's Introduction:
   Air Chief Marshal Sir John Barraclough
3. Setting the Scene: Mr. John Terraine
4. The Organisation, Structure and Tasks of Coastal Command:
   Air Vice-Marshal W. Oulton
5. The Course of the Battle: Lt. Commander W. J. R. Gardner
6. Intelligence: Mr. Edward Thomas
7. Development of Equipment and Techniques: Dr. Alfred Price
8. A German Perspective: Dr. J. Rohwer
9. Pre-lunch Discussion
10. Digest of the Group Discussions
    A. Policies, Priorities and Politics
    B. Coastal Command, Operations, Techniques and Equipment
    C. Intelligence
    D. Maritime/Air Doctrine and Policy
    E. German Operations and Equipment
11. Lessons for the Present: Air Marshal Sir John Curtiss
12. Closing Remarks by the Chairman RAF Historical Society
    Biographical Notes on the Main Speakers
    Addendum
    The Royal Air Force Historical Society
    Acknowledgement

Preface

To commemorate the Battle of the Atlantic 50 years on, the RAF Historical Society and the RAF Staff College convened a joint seminar at Bracknell on 21 October 1991. This was the second in an on-going series of seminars under the general title of the Bracknell Papers.

The audience of just under 300 consisted of some 100 members of the RAF Historical Association and the Bracknell Directing Staff and students.

Contributions were made by some 50 former RAF and Royal Navy officers, including a number of historians of both light and dark blue origin. A German view of the Battle was represented by an eminent German historian.

The day's proceedings were presided over by Air Chief Marshal Sir John Barraclough and a similar pattern to the Battle of Britain symposium in 1990 was followed.

The morning was devoted to a series of six talks on various aspects of the Battle, while in the afternoon the symposium was divided into discussion groups in which issues raised were debated in more detail. These provided an opportunity for Battle of the Atlantic veterans and others to offer recollections and for historians to comment further on various questions and controversies. The day's events were rounded off with an address by Air Marshal Sir John Curtiss.

This volume contains the edited texts of the main talks and a digest of what was said in the discussion groups.

Derek Wood
Editor

"We who dwell, in the British Isles must celebrate with joy and thankfulness our deliverance from the mortal U-boat perils, which deliverance lighteth the year which has ended. When I look back upon the fifty-five months of this hard and obstinate war, which makes ever more exacting demands upon our life's springs of energy and contrivance, I still rate highest among the dangers we have to overcome the U-boat attack on our shipping, without which we cannot live or even receive the help which our Dominions and our grand and generous American ally have sent us."

Signed by the Prime Minister, Winston Churchill

The original of the above was given to Air Marshal Sir Edward Chilton, A-O-C-in-C. RAF Coastal Command.

It was framed and hung in the Officers' Mess at Northwood, but unfortunately was destroyed in the great fire there. It formed part of a speech which Winston Churchill made in April 1944.

Back – Left to Right
Air Chief Marshal Sir Neville Stack, Air Marshal Sir Frederick Sowrey

Front – Left to Right
Air Marshal Sir Edward Chilton, Lord Shackleton.

1. Opening Remarks

The Commandant
Air Vice-Marshal R. G. Peters

It is my very great pleasure on behalf of all those resident at the college to bid a warm welcome to our visitors to this second RAF Historical Society Symposium on Second World War anniversaries. I know that many of you have been eagerly awaiting today and many have travelled far to be here. I trust you will not be disappointed and will have a thundering good day.

This symposium has, I am delighted to say, proved very popular and there is one drawback, that we have too many people to accommodate in the one lecture hall, and we have had to make use of the Salmond Room for a CCTV link. I hope those of you there will feel fully part of the proceedings.

Last year's very successful symposium was on the Battle of Britain; next year in March we shall be holding one on the development of land/air warfare and the war in the Mediterranean and the North African littoral. For me these symposia give not only the chance to look back in history and project from that to the future but also an opportunity to ensure a vital interaction between people of all ages and experiences. For some of you who are veterans of the Battle of the Atlantic today may be a chance for some nostalgia and a chance to meet old friends. For the historians it may be an opportunity to argue your particular point or line – and I trust to ensure our accuracy; for the members of the Staff College course it is an opportunity to look at a major element of the Second World War and to participate in living history. Sadly the pressures of the syllabus these days prevent us looking at such events in quite the detail that might be desirable, so I am particularly glad that we are able to combine with the RAF Historical Society in this series of symposia and to allow the course members to mix with you, learn from you, and I hope in turn to give you something of their experience and knowledge of the modern Air Force and the way it's working.

Normally on these occasions it is my lot to introduce speakers and moderate affairs. Today I am happy to report that we have someone infinitely better qualified: Air Chief Marshal Sir John Barraclough. He was commissioned in 1938 and served during the Second World War in Coastal Command and later in the Middle East Air Force, he took part in the campaign in Madagascar and commanded the captured Italian airfield at Mogadishu. After the war he commanded RAF Biggin Hill and RAF Middleton-St George, known to some of us these days as Teeside Airport. He also served in FEAF, and as AOC 19 Gp; he was VCDS, Air Secretary and finally Commandant RCDS. Since retirement he has been active in many defence matters and has also been Chairman of the Commonwealth War Graves Commission and Inspector General of the RAuxAF. He is extremely well qualified, by experience and capability, to run our affairs today.

2. Chairman's Introduction

Air Chief Marshal Sir John Barraclough

A very warm thanks to our invited guest speakers, who are giving up their time to making this day possible. We are most appreciative of the hospitality and facilities of the College. Our Chairman will speak of this later in the day, but I should here like to register our appreciation of his initiative, vision and drive in founding our RAFHS some five years ago. What a success it has been. All of us who hold our Service dear and see the importance of its history when recalled in tranquillity have reason to thank Sir Freddie, his Committee and his helpers for all that they have done and continue to do in that cause, and I hope words to that affect can be included in the proceedings of this day. The thrust of this symposium is of course the anti-submarine war, and for this morning we must confine it to that. But in seminars the anti-shipping, mining and other exciting things that happened at sea can, of course, be considered.

Our first speaker is Mr John Terraine, a most eminent historian, broadcaster and writer on military matters – and most recently on RAF and maritime matters. His contributions to the literature have been most justly recognised by the highest awards and distinctions, and we are very fortunate to have him set the scene for us. He will be followed by Air Vice-Marshal Wilf Oulton, who took part in every aspect of the battle, as aircraft captain, squadron commander, station commander – with land and sea planes – and was then on the staff. He will tell us of the wartime tasks and structure of Coastal Command. I think Staff College students will find interesting anomalies in both. Lieutenant Commander Jock Gardner – naval historian and anti-submarine warfare specialist – will then give us a sharply focussed retrospect on the course of the battle, and Mr Edward Thomas, a guru from that secret world of Bletchley and naval intelligence – will fill in the intelligence background (perhaps it was the foreground on some occasions, for what an intelligence driven war it turned out to be).

Dr Alfred Price will next take up the story. He flew with the V Force as an AEO and later became an air historian – a prolific writer on air matters, and producer of highly regarded works. He will talk about the equipment and the techniques that went with them. I am reminded that in the earlier grey-water days of the war those of us that were flying biplane flying boats over the North Sea had no intercom since none was installed; other than the message pad which we sometimes proffered to the next crew member on a pair of home-made calipers, or an electric bell system which we bought locally and installed ourselves. That was how we communicated – the present generation will find it scarcely credible. Two rings on the bell meant 'Action Stations' whereas one might mean just another cup of tea for the Captain.

To round off this panoply of views we are fortunate indeed to have with us, to give a German perspective, Professor Jurgen Rohwer, who served in the German Navy during the war and went on to become one of his country's leading authorities on the war at sea as historian and author. Herr Professor, we very much value having you with us today and are greatly looking forward to having your insight into the other side – or 'the underside' - of the story.

Then to help us this afternoon we have with us some who took part in the battle. It is nice to be able to welcome Lord Shackleton, a dedicated Coastal Command intelligence officer who went on to high political office but has never flagged in his interest and support of our Service and of Coastal Command in particular. A great welcome goes too to Sir Edward Chilton, in many ways the embodiment of Coastal Command, one of our great experts on maritime air war, and also on the Royal Navy, Air Marshal Sir John Curtiss, commander of 18 Group during the Falklands Conflict, is also here, and will address us later in the afternoon. I see many other old friends, and if the RAF Historical Society did nothing more than bring so many friends together it would be a terrific achievement. I must stop name-dropping except to say how good it is to see Sqn Ldr Terry Bulloch, the famed captain of that famed Liberator of 120 Squadron which attracted U-boats as moths are attracted to candles, to the admiration of all of us and the envy of most of us who had to make do with a diet of occasionally disappearing radar contacts.

3. Setting the Scene

Mr. John Terraine

The Battle of the Atlantic, properly speaking, began in June 1940 and ended in May 1943. I expressed the opinion, in THE RIGHT OF THE LINE, that "of all the battles of the Second World War, it is impossible to think of one more momentous than the Atlantic victory". I have never felt any inclination to depart from that view.

The time-span, however, indicates quite clearly that, historically, this great, costly and still under-valued contest really only supplies the stupendous, central climax of the submarine – and, by the same token, the anti-submarine – wars. Submarine warfare in both its aspects overlapped the Atlantic battle at each end.

At the core of it is technology. It is a simple fact, unfortunately obscured for a critical period, that both the submarine wars (comprising our entire experience of such things) belong to the same bracket of technology. They used the same sort of machines, the same sort of weapons, and the same techniques, barring only natural improvements under the stress of war and one notable innovation. And the 'nature of the beast' was bluntly declared right at the beginning.

Submarine warfare quickly announced itself as trade war, a new and very deadly version of the ancient practice of blockade. The first merchant ship to be sunk by a submarine was a small British steamer sent to the bottom by U 17 on 20 October 1914; on that occasion the crew was saved by the chivalry of the U-boat commander. Six days later, however, on 26 October, U 24 established an even more significant 'first': a French vessel carrying about 2,500 Belgian refugees, torpedoed without any warning, and this time there was no chivalry – about 40 lives were lost. 'Unrestricted Submarine Warfare' had made its appearance, though it did not become normal procedure until later, and was not openly affirmed until 1 February 1917. Thereafter, with or without declaration, submarine warfare was always 'unrestricted', a fact made very plain by the sinking of the liner Athenia by U 30 on 3 September 1939, the very first day of World War II.

Before going any further, I think I should say a few words about machines and weapons. First, the basic machine of the two submarine wars: this was, of course, the so-called submarine itself, the German U-boat. I say 'so-called' because, from August 1914 until nearly the end of 1944, all the underwater craft employed were really 'submersibles'. True submarines did not appear until the 1950s, with the advent of nuclear propulsion which gave them high performance submerged as well as on the surface and enabled them to remain submerged for indefinite periods. In 1944 the Schnorkel device made possible an approach to true submarine characteristics which threatened to cancel out all the hard-won advantages which had produced the Atlantic victory. This grim prospect was averted just in time by Germany's collapse. The victory itself was thus won against submersibles which came in a direct line of descent from the U-boats of 1914-18; indeed, the U 105-114 type which appeared in June 1918 bore an amazingly close resemblance to the Type VII which was Germany's main operational U-boat from 1939-45. From this descended the long-range Type IX and the Type XIV tankers; they all belonged to the same family.

Anti-submarine machines did not exist in 1914. They were something that had to be born of the war itself, but by 1918 they were various and impressive. In both wars, the U-boat's main enemy was the destroyer, and one may note that the anti-submarine role was in flat contradiction to the destroyer's chief intended characteristic – speed. By comparison with what destroyers were meant to do, anti-submarine warfare was slow work – but rarely dull. By 1918 the Royal Navy's first specifically anti-submarine craft appeared - "Flower" Class sloops built on merchant-ship lines with speeds of $16\frac{1}{2}$-$17\frac{1}{2}$ knots. One hundred and twelve of these were launches, predecessors of a second "Flower" Class which made its appearance in 1940 under the revived – and misleading – name of 'corvette'. These were to be the "Work-horses of the Atlantic Battle", and the parents of what were sometimes called 'super-corvettes', but usually – and also misleadingly - 'frigates'. They were just becoming an important element as the Battle entered its final stage in 1943. And in that year, too, we find another purpose-built type becoming effective after a long wait – the escort aircraft-carrier.

1914 was the start-line of an unprecedented period of innovation in war. At the top of the list of novelties, alongside submarine warfare there came air warfare, both creating entirely new dimensions of conflict. The aircraft of 1914 were primitive and feeble, but war brings all technology on very fast, and by 1917 maritime aviation, conducted by the Royal Naval Air Service, was an established element of anti-U-boat warfare, using normal land-based machines and some specialities. Airships were found to be more useful over water than over land (and continued to be so used in World War II), flying-boats were invaluable for extended patrols, especially in the North Sea, flying the famous 'Spider's Web' patrol pattern which was revived in 1944 for the protection of the D-Day armada, and seaplanes, which carried the main burden of war against the U-boats. Both of these types were forerunners: the F2 Felixstowe flying boat of 1918 was the precursor of the splendid Short Sunderland of 1939-45, and according to Owen Thetford the Short Type 184 torpedo-carrying seaplane of 1915 "was to the First World War what the Swordfish became in the Second".

It is now established that only one U-boat was definitely sunk by aircraft between 1914 and 1918. The air contribution was deterrent, rather than lethal, but as I shall indicate – and most merchant seamen would confirm – there is nothing at all wrong with that. By November 1918 the maritime strength of what was now the RAF was 43 squadrons and 7 independent flights, a total of 685 aircraft plus 103 airships; 37 squadrons out of the 43 were engaged in anti-U-boat duties. It comes as a shock to find that in 1939 Coastal Command had no anti-submarine role at all; but in May 1943, as the Battle of the Atlantic reached its climax, thanks to never-resting technology Coastal Command was a prime U-boat killer.

I am not going to say very much now about weapons, but they are central to our subject – indeed, technique is meaningless without reference to them. World War I displayed the main pointer of submarine warfare weaponry; World War II produced a diversity which was far from complete when the Atlantic battle ended and included at the very end revolutionary new types of submarine which, as I said, could well have reversed the result. Meanwhile, in both the 'submersible' wars, the weapon of 'unrestricted' warfare was undoubtedly the torpedo, and despite some artistic variations the most effective of them in terms of shipping tonnage sunk was the standard 21-inch model. U-boats also used mines, guns and (for self-defence) anti-aircraft guns; but everything that is implied in the word 'unrestricted' is due to the devastating nature of the torpedo.

For attacking submarines, it was clearly established by 1918 that the weapon of the future was the depth charge. First thought of in 1911, they did not become available until 1916; in 1917 a ship's normal depth charge equipment was four, but in 1918 it had increased to between 30 and 50, which was standard in World War II. The great advance of World War II was the airborne depth charge, which gave Coastal Command the lethal weapon it totally lacked at the outbreak of war. Yet its fruition was delayed for as long as the original development had been in the previous war. Thanks to the Operational Research Unit set up by Sir Philip Joubert in 1941, and its scientific study of airborne depth charge attacks, Coastal Command became a true U-boat-fighting instrument in July 1942 – the month of its first sinking – and never looked back.

Let us now consider what were the objects of the exercise in this hard cruel struggle. What do phrases like 'trade war', 'unrestricted war' mean? Admiral Dönitz, the World War II U-boat commander, was perfectly clear about what he was trying to do. He was trying to cut off the supplies of food, raw materials and manufactured goods (especially weapons) without which Britain would have to surrender. He was playing for the jackpot. His philosophy was simple, and applied to the whole British merchant marine and all its allies and associates; he expressed it in these words:

"The enemy's shipping constitutes one single, great entity. It is therefore immaterial where a ship is sunk. Once it has been destroyed it has to be replaced by a new ship, and that's that."

It was brutally simple: "Sink ships, and go on sinking ships." Just that.

What was the appropriate reply, then? The one that sprang immediately to mind, and does seem to offer every satisfaction, was "sink U-boats, the more the better", and in both wars this was the most-favoured programme of anti-submarine warfare. Great store was set from the very beginning by what were called 'offensive patrols', or 'hunting groups', preferably with an air component, whose task would be to hunt U-boats to the death wherever they might be found. But there lay the rub. The U-boats' prime characteristic was their ability to become invisible. Most of the time, they couldn't be found.

By 1918, however, the answer to this conundrum was quite

clear, to those with eyes to see. With our gift of hindsight, it seems obvious that the U-boat could almost always be found, sooner or later, in the proximity of the merchant ships that it had to sink. In 1917 these were grouped in escorted convoys, and submarine warfare assumed a new dimension which swung the advantage for a time towards the defence. The 1917-18 U-boats did not evolve a system for successful attack on convoys, and certainly not for convoys with air escort as well as naval. In 1918 only three ships were sunk from convoys which had air escort, and the correct manner of employment was well understood. The true assessment of the role of convoy took a long time to sink in. We have to remember that Operational Research was in its very infancy in World War I, with the result, very clearly spelt out by the American historian of the Royal Navy, Professor A J Marder, in the 1960s and '70s, that:

"The Admiralty did not understand that an increase in convoys meant an increase in opportunities to attack U-boats, and therefore more U-boats destroyed; nor that if it was a fine thing to dispose of a U-boat, it was even better to keep them down and thus bring the convoy to harbour without loss."

This lesson took until 1941 to penetrate; it was in April of that year that Western Approaches Command issued its famous convoy instruction stating:

"The safe and timely arrival of the convoy at its destination is the primary object, and nothing releases the escort commander of his responsibility in this respect."

Professor Marder goes even further; he says:

"The merits of convoy can be argued cogently without the question of sinking submarines ever coming into it. Sinking submarines is a bonus, not a necessity ... what matters is that the ships deliver cargoes regularly and adequately ..."

And he carries the argument even further than that; he adds

"It really did not matter how many U-boats the Germans had, if they were forced to keep out of the way and the British and their Allies got their ships with their literally vital cargoes through ..."

Here, I think, he is too dismissive. How do you force a U-boat to 'keep out of the way'? Surely the only sound method is by sinking so many that the rest become too discouraged to attack, which was palpably what was happening in May 1943. But all the rest of Professor Marder's analysis seems to me to be indisputable; defending convoys was the best way to sink U-boats, and the 'bonus' was worth having. The attack on convoys and their defence composed the main tactical scenario of the Battle of the Atlantic. It was a product of the 'Dönitz System' - that amazing system of remote personal tactical control of battle made possible by the great advances of wireless technology between the wars. This was what made possible the formation of 'U-boat packs' whose onslaught on convoys could be devastating, not least in the early days of the battle in the autumn of 1940. The habitual U-boat tactic against convoys was one already adopted in 1918: they attacked on the surface, at night, and this threw the defending forces into great confusion for some time. By attacking on the surface, they nullified the ASDIC (Sonar) detection on which the Royal Navy entirely relied, and the cover of darkness ruled out air detection. So the U-boats enjoyed what they called a 'happy time', the Royal Navy bit its lips on a lot of chagrin, the Merchant Navy suffered some heavy losses and the RAF endured a great deal of frustration. The solution to the problem – in technology's fullness of time – would be radar, shipborne and airborne, against which darkness gave no cover. This was the 'notable innovation' that I spoke of earlier.

In my book BUSINESS IN GREAT WATERS I have dwelt upon the strange dual nature of the Atlantic battle. It was fought right across the North Atlantic, deep into the South, with U-boats operating in the Mediterranean and the Indian Ocean, but with its control centre as far away as Lorient, and then Berlin. This separation of command and performance seems to go against all the principles of war, and naval war not least. In 1942 it came to its high peak, with 7,790,697 tons of shipping – 1,664 ships – sunk: of this terrible total, U-boats were responsible for 6,266,215 tons – 1,160 ships – and no less than 5,471,222 tons – 1,006 ships – were lost in the North Atlantic. This was the ripe fruit of the Dönitz system.

But now the astonishing armoury of anti-submarine warfare was moving towards completion, and Professor Jurgen Rohwer, whom we are fortunate to have with us today, has said that in fact the crisis of the Atlantic Battle had already passed. The Dönitz system contained its own in-built weakness: the volume of radio signals required to make it function. The monitoring and decryption of enemy radio signals dated from the earliest days of August 1914, and R M Grant, in his book U-BOAT INTELLIGENCE, says flatly,

"For the anti-submarine war of 1914-18 [decryption] was perhaps the most significant contributor to British and Allied victory." Professor Rohwer has supplied the World War II sequel to that statement:

"During the second half year of 1941, by a very cautious estimate the Submarine Tracking Room of the Admiralty, using ULTRA decrypts, re-routed the convoys so cleverly around the German 'wolf-packs' that about 300 ships were saved by avoiding battles. They seem to me more decisive to the outcome of the Battle [of the Atlantic] than the U-boats sunk in the convoy battles of 1943 or in the Bay offensives."

Professor Rohwer will no doubt wish to expound that thought.

It remains, nevertheless, to note that the convoy battles of 1943 are a fact embodying some remarkable history, not least for Coastal Command. It was, indeed, this Command which was responsible for the battle being fought right across the Atlantic instead of, as in World War I, in British home waters. Air power, in its deterrent, or 'Scarecrow', role, steadily forced the U-boats out further and further westward until they were out of its own reach. There then followed that somewhat unedifying struggle for the very long range (VLR) aircraft (and especially the Consolidated B-24s best known in their maritime appearance as 'Liberators'), which alone could cover the dreaded 'Atlantic Gap'. But meanwhile the Allied Air Forces, Coastal Command, Bomber Command, US Navy and US Army and Fleet Air Arm, had moved to centre stage in the fight against U-boats at the 'sharp end'. In the second half of 1942 their combined sinkings of U-boats averaged almost 50% of the total, and in the final month of May 1943 the average climbed to over 52%; well might one U-boat captain say,

"The British ruled the sky."

The U-boat wars were, as I said, governed by technology, and it was a combination of technologies that brought victory: VLR aircraft, depth charges, homing torpedoes, escort carriers, ULTRA decrypts, D/F fixes, HF/DF fixes, ASDIC, radar, multiple bomb-throwers, each at its appointed time.

As I said at the beginning, it is impossible to think of a victory more momentous than the one in the Atlantic. That is not meant to be merely a well-deserved tribute to all the courage and resolution that had gone into it; it is a recognition that the nature of the Battle had totally changed in 1941. No longer was it a fight for Britain's survival, a defensive victory; it had also become an intrinsic part of the main offensive strategy of the Second World War. For the Western Allies, by solemn agreement, the supreme offensive action was Operation OVERLORD, the re-entry into north-western Europe. That vast enterprise could not have taken place without this Atlantic victory, to which Coastal Command made such a magnificent contribution.

4. Organisation, Structure and Tasks of Coastal Command

Air Vice-Marshal W. Oulton

The organisation and disposition of the elements of Coastal Command at the outbreak of war in September 1939 reflect the tasks which it was expected to perform in support of the Navy. These in turn derived from the Admiralty's view of the likely course of the war at sea. With great confidence in the effectiveness of ASDIC, they at first regarded the U-boat as a relatively minor problem; their chief concern was with the activities of the enemy's surface ships. The primary task of Coastal Command was therefore to search for and report the positions of any enemy ships trying to break out of the North Sea into the open Atlantic. A secondary role was the provision of escort to coastal convoys.

Coastal Command with its HQ at Northwood, to which it had recently moved so as to be near the Admiralty as well as Bomber and Fighter Commands, therefore deployed its forces through two east-facing Group headquarters, No 16 Group at Chatham near the Naval C-in-C Nore, and No 18 Group at Donibristle in southern Scotland. All except three of the Command's front-line squadrons were based on airfields facing the North Sea or the eastern Channel.

AOC-in-C Coastal had for long been convinced that the U-boat would be a much greater threat than the Admiralty supposed and a new Group HQ, No 15, had been formed at Mount Batten, Plymouth, with two flying boat squadrons – one at Mount Batten, one at Pembroke Dock – and an Auxiliary Air Force Anson squadron in Northern Ireland (Aldergrove). These were tasked to provide a modicum of anti-U-boat protection to the mass of shipping arriving from the west and were soon reinforced by 217 (Anson) squadron moving from Tangmere to Warmwell and Carew Cheriton.

To perform all these tasks, Coastal had a total of sixteen squadrons, four of flying boats, one of elderly bi-plane torpedo bombers and the rest General Reconnaissance landplanes, Ansons and Hudsons. None of them had any effective means of attacking anything. All this amounted to a total of 180 front-line aircraft plus 60 in immediate reserve.

During the first seven months or so, the patrolling of the North Sea was largely ineffective – the GRAF SPEE and the DEUTSCHLAND had already been in the Atlantic. It was the sinking of the ATHENIA and various other ships that foretold the real war at sea. Then with the fall of Norway, followed by that of France in mid-1940, the whole picture was dramatically changed. U-boats operating from French ports were now poised to cut off the seaborne supply line on which our immediate existence depended, and on which any continuation of the war and any ultimate victory equally depended.

Initially the losses of merchant shipping – and the precious supplies of fuel, food and munitions which they carried – were horrendous. Bitter experience soon taught that the safe and timely arrival of any convoy – or even fast independent ships – required close co-operation between Coastal Command and the Admiralty, between regional naval Cs-in-C and their local maritime Group HQ, between ships and aircraft. 15 Group moved from Plymouth to Liverpool – Derby House – to work intimately alongside the new Naval C-in-C Western Approaches, and a new group, No 19, formed at Plymouth to work alongside C-in-C Plymouth covering the south-western approaches and the northern Bay of Biscay. A new Air HQ was formed at Gibraltar, functioning as a group HQ, covering the southern Bay and the Straits, and another Air HQ was formed in Iceland. This operated Hudson aircraft at first and then much later the precious squadron of Liberator aircraft which, with their much greater range and endurance, made such a vital difference to north-routed convoys.

At one time in 1940, when things had been going badly for the Admiralty, they demanded – as on so many other occasions – to take over Coastal Command and incorporate it in the Navy, which would have been disastrous. Fortunately, the Cabinet Defence Committee, overcome by a sudden attack of common-sense, very wisely decided to leave Coastal Command in the RAF for training, equipping, administration and day-to-day operations, but it would execute tasks as laid down broadly by the Admiralty. This in fact was what had been happening all along so the decision made no discernible difference.

On the other side of the Atlantic, under the control of the Joint

HQ at Halifax, Nova Scotia, the Royal Canadian Navy and Air Force provided convoy escort and cover out to similar limits. The map shows the limits of the air cover which could be provided and it was in the gap in the middle that the U-boats inflicted such heavy losses. Whenever a long range Liberator from Iceland could reach some part of the gap, the losses for the moment were negligible.

To enable the massive supply operation necessary for the re-entry into France to proceed, it was essential to close this mid-Atlantic gap and so in October 1943 Coastal Command established a base in the Azores. On the first operational sortie a U-boat was sunk. That, combined with spectacular success by the USS BOGUE, a "Tupperware" aircraft carrier, effectively closed the gap.

During these years, Coastal Command, with its HQ at North-wood, grew in size, efficiency and scope, exercising its control and authority – through Group and Air Headquarters – over airfields and flying boat bases running from Iceland through the Hebrides and the whole of the UK and Northern Ireland to Gibraltar and on as far as Freetown on the coast of West Africa.

It was fortunate to have incorporated into the staff strong and very co-operative Naval liaison – in the form of that splendid man Captain Peyton-Ward. At the same time it acquired other responsibilities, such as air-sea rescue, which initially had been completely neglected, and the vital but largely unrecognised Photographic Reconnaissance.

No improvement in organisation, however, was of the slightest use if we did not have the aircraft and the weapons. Once away from the narrow confines of the North Sea, the Anson was almost useless. The flying boats were far too few in number and the rate of production was much too low. A few Catalinas were brought in and did sterling work, but they again were too few and often too slow when it came to attacking U-boats. The only solution was to divert bomber aircraft from the direct offensive against Germany to the task of ensuring the arrival of the supplies needed to keep that offensive going at all. Inevitably there were terrible political battles over priorities and only very grudgingly were some few bombers released to Coastal. Two squadrons of Whitleys arrived at first, replaced by Halifaxes later; next came two squadrons of Lease-Lend B 17s and one precious squadron's worth of Very Long Range B 24 Liberators, with a second squadron later on. Then came Wellingtons equipped with the famous Leigh Light, which made night attacks possible. Credit must also be given to the brave efforts of 10 OTU.

It was not only the aircraft, of course. There were equally bitter struggles to get some of the new electronic equipment, particularly the improved radars, to make the aircraft effective. As for weapons, Coastal helped itself. The special anti-submarine bombs proved useless, and through the local initiative of a flight commander the standard naval depth charge was adapted and then improved, and it became for a long time the principal weapon. It must be admitted, however, that we did eventually get a specialised homing torpedo, which did very well. But all of this was just making do with what could be made available. At no stage of the war did Coastal Command have an aircraft designed and equipped purposely for anti-submarine warfare.

Nevertheless it must be recognised that the VLR Liberator made a very good anti-submarine aircraft, particularly after it was fitted with the Leigh Light, so well proved in operations by Wellington squadrons. The RAF never got enough of them, but US Navy and Army Air Force squadrons with the same aircraft came and made a most valuable contribution to the task.

So, to revert to the title of this paper, what were the tasks of Coastal Command? The first and overriding priority was to assure, both independently and in co-operation with naval forces, the safe arrival of shipping. This in turn became primarily defence against the U-boat by convoy escort and by destruction of U-boats in transit to and from their operational areas. But it also involved searching for enemy surface forces, as originally required by the Admiralty, and the location of the Bismarck, a terrifying threat to our shipping in the Atlantic, was by a Coastal Command Catalina flying boat. At one time location and destruction of mines in shipping channels was an additional important task. Photographic reconnaissance of some distant targets, as I have already mentioned, was another important task, although not always recognised as being very relevant to the Battle of the Atlantic.

The epitome of the defence against U-boats came with Operation CORK – the shutting out of all U-boats from entry to the English Channel during OVERLORD – the invasion of Normandy on 6 June 1944. Although many tried valiantly, not one U-boat got through to attack the solid mass of cross-Channel shipping on that fateful day. That was the time when, on a bright moonlight night, Flying Officer Moore in his Liberator sank two U-boats in 20 minutes as they tried to dash through to attack the invasion fleet.

So, having begun the war with the wrong aircraft, inadequately equipped, with the wrong aim, and with crews incorrectly trained, Coastal ended the war on a note of some satisfaction, with nearly a thousand well equipped aircraft, and well-trained and experienced crews capable in every maritime air role. But it was well for us that the war finished when it did, for the scene was about to change dramatically with an imminent great leap forward in submarine technology. But that subject I leave to another speaker.

5. *The Course of the Battle*

Lt. Commander W. J. R. Gardner

On 3 September 1939 the German submarine U-30 sank the 14,000 ton liner *Athenia:* the much smaller *Avondale Park* was despatched by U-2336 on 7 May 1945, arguably the last victim of the conflict. The losses of these merchant ships signify the length of the conflict; the other immediate dimension to consider is that of shipping tonnage lost. The North Atlantic saw the sinking of some 14 million tons of ships, that is a thousand *Athenias or* about 5,000 *Avondale Parks by* submarine alone. This total was achieved by a maximum of about 460 submarines[1]. By the end of the war, these were opposed by around 900 ASW vessels which were under British operational command and about 700 aircraft belonging to Coastal Command.

In such a short paper it is first important to introduce some limitations of scope. The first has already been hinted at; the area is confined to the North Atlantic, where the shipping battle was concentrated. Intense and often strategically important activities in the Norwegian Sea, Arctic Ocean and, above all, the Mediterranean are not described. Secondly, as the submarine was responsible for some 63% of all losses (including marine accidents), no account is taken of the losses caused by mines, coastal forces, surface raiders or air attacks on shipping.

In this paper, a broadly chronological approach will be taken working through from beginning to end but taking several stops along the way to allow discussion of particular themes. During such diversions it may be necessary to consider a greater span of time than that which strictly belongs to the stopping point; further it may be necessary to go backwards, as well as forwards, to explore the topic.

Three broad periods will be investigated; obviously, no complete narrative can be presented, but a flavour of each portion of time will be conveyed. In discussing the topics, the most significant factors in the conduct and outcome of the battle will be brought out; but, quite deliberately, no attempt will be made to put them in any order of significance. On the other hand, successes and failures, strengths and weaknesses of strategy, tactics, technique and equipment should become evident.

As a last introductory point, it is important to distinguish variations in aims and methods adopted by the two sides. On land – sometimes even in the air – there tends to a divergency of aim, usually in connection with a single area or parcel of air.

Things happen rather differently at sea, and it is not necessarily important to have absolute control over a patch of water, in order to attain important, even essential, aims. Thus, it can be argued that with the possible exception of the very last period of the campaign, neither side had absolute control.

That said, it is fairly easy to identify the aim of each side. In the Allied case it was quite simply to ensure the prompt and sufficient arrival of the necessary level of supply in order, firstly, to guarantee national survival and secondly, to facilitate the desired level of military operations. This was a constant aim, whose contributory methods were altered and improved as the campaign progressed, without prejudice to the end.

At first inspection, it would appear that the Germans possessed the same unity of purpose with the aim being to sink the maximum tonnage of Allied merchant shipping but it can be argued that subsequent shifts of method were sufficiently fundamental to effect a shift in aim. This paper is not the place to explore this fascinating topic in detail; but three distinct phases, not necessarily corresponding exactly to the periods of this account, can be identified. In the first, the leading theme is that of improvisation, the Kriegsmarine in general and the submarine arm in particular having neither the quantity or quality of warships and equipment desired for maritime conflict with Great Britain, far less any actual or potential allies. During the second period, the tonnage war seemed to predominate in most strategic and tactical calculations: some reservations must be drawn as to the constancy of this concept at the grand strategic level, which is here taken to mean beyond the German Navy, in the realms of other services, especially the Luftwaffe; and at the highest level of national command – Adolf Hitler[2]. Thirdly, a rationale was adopted latterly of conducting a submarine campaign against shipping, not to maximise sinkings, but simply to divert as much of the Allied war effort away from other things as possible. Although there is some justification for Dönitz's supporting assertion that the forces required for effective ASW are of a much greater order than that required for a submarine campaign, some of his statistics are suspect: perhaps more importantly, in terms of economic warfare, these large scale ASW expenditures were well within Allied capacities.

Although a three part distinction of German aims has been drawn, these do not correspond exactly with the three phases to be adopted in describing the campaign. It is proposed to split the battle thus:

- From the outbreak of war until the end of 1941 and the full entry of the USA into the war.

- From the beginning of 1942 to the middle of 1943.

- From the middle of 1943 until the end.

BEGINNINGS: SEPTEMBER 1939 – DECEMBER 1941

As described in the introduction, the loss of the *Athenia* occurred at a very early stage. At this point it was not the intention of the German High Command to engage in total war, and this sinking was an embarrassment to them[3]. The restrictions on the U-boat captains both before and after this event indicate the reluctance to engage in war *a l'outrance*. In any case, there were few boats deployed.

The total numbers were, in any case, far short of the 300 stated by Dönitz as his requirement for such a campaign. He had made out such a case[4], making the assumptions that German operations against shipping would have to be routed via the north of Scotland and that a convoy system would be rapidly instituted. Both of these reflected the initial situation, and he thus found himself far short of his requirements. To make matters worse, there were considerable problems with the reliability of torpedoes, a matter not rectified for some time. The sum of these limitations constrained the potential of the U-boats considerably.

But it must not be assumed that all these difficulties ensured immunity for allied shipping. In the four months of war in 1939 alone, about a million tons was lost, some four fifths of this figure being due to enemy action, rather than marine accident. It should be remembered that the merchant vessel of this era was very much smaller than today's bulk carrier or container ship. On the positive side for the Allies, the convoy system was instituted early although not to the extent that was considered desirable. There were significant exclusions, principally on certain routes, with vessels of some nationalities and of the fastest and slowest vessels. The band of ship speeds considered for convoying varied throughout the war, and attempts were made to broaden the range, as well as the routes, as much as possible.

At this point, it is helpful to consider the advantages given to convoyed shipping. Contrary to some popular belief, convoy started not in the Second World War, or even in the prior conflict between 1914 and 1918, but several centuries earlier. Spanish plate was convoyed from the Americas in the days of Drake, and the technique was in common use in Nelson's era. The system has two main beneficial characteristics;

- The concentration by area of targets, making open ocean reconnaissance more difficult.

- The stationing of escorts in the vicinity of the submarine's targets, increasing the probability that an engagement may occur.

- In theoretical discussion, these benefits may often appear to be obscured by two false premises;

- The fallacy that ships are protecting area, and not shipping.

- The drawing, or at least the inappropriate application, of distinctions between offensive and defensive measures.

The institution of convoy was broadly successful in as much as it caused submarines to look to ships sailing independently for targets, thus permitting the large numbers under escort to pass relatively unmolested.

There were, however, only a relatively small number of escorts available. Such a situation existed partly because rearmament had not yet fully developed: the British (and French) were little more prepared for war in 1939 than the U-boats. Further, there were widespread commitments for the existing fleet. These ranged from the North Cape to the South Atlantic; from Canada to the Far East. The considerable force of battleships and aircraft-carriers needed the type of ships in support which were the only conceivable ocean convoy escorts, at least until significant numbers of specialist vessels could be built. Operations such as those in Norway not only absorbed destroyers[5], they also tended to result in sinking and damage to these vessels. After the fall of France in mid-1940, very significant numbers of these ships were required to be kept close to Britain, as an anti-invasion measure: it was not until the threat receded that these could be returned to convoy duties.

Destroyers, in the form in which they entered the war, were not necessarily ideal for ASW. Qualities such as high speed, heavy gun and torpedo armament were more in evidence rather than endurance – especially in heavy weather – and large anti-submarine armament. Such attributes also ensured that these ships would be required for virtually every form of maritime warfare: convoy escort might be important, but it was not the only priority.

But perhaps it was in the field of sensors, that they were most deficient, especially at the outset of the campaign. An almost touching confidence in ASDIC had given a false sense of confidence suggesting that submarines were unlikely to prove any form of significant threat. Certain trials had suggested that ASDIC might be highly effective, but this was bounded greatly both by weather conditions and – at least as importantly – variations in seawater. Oceanography, as it would now be called, was by no means as well understood as it is now. Such utility as ASDIC might have had was to some extent discounted by German thinking on attack tactics, which had taken this development into account. They considered that it might well be difficult to reach attacking positions fully submerged, and thus susceptible to ASDIC detection, and planned, wherever possible to attack semi-surfaced – and therefore invulnerable to ASDIC – preferably at night. This tactic was to reach its greatest point of refinement when used by groups of submarines against convoys later in the war.

In this early stage, it was difficult to produce any form of counter to such a tactic. A partly submerged submarine made a very small visual target and surface ships, especially relatively large merchant vessels, could be seen from much further away than the submarine could, particularly at night. Radar was not to be immediately available or widely fitted in this period[6].

Nor was all satisfactory in the air. The Royal Navy initially made no significant use of aircraft in the war against submarines. The Royal Air Force was not prepared for the immediate problem or the battle that ensued. There was a paucity of both equipment and aircraft suitable for the task. Airborne radar was still some way off, and search capability was confined to the eye, obviously only effective by day. There was no weapon truly suitable for engaging a submarine unless it co-operated by staying on the surface to be bombed: better weapons were to be introduced fairly quickly but problems of aiming and depth setting were to persist for some time. But one of the greatest advantages of the aircraft in ASW lies not just in an ability to attack submarines, but also in the large amount of water that it can search in a relatively short time; and the resultant deterrent, or at least irritant, effect on submarine operations. But even here, all was not well. There were only a very few aircraft and, in general terms, these had insufficient range to be effective. It would be easy, obvious and wrong to lay the blame for this unpreparedness entirely at the feet of the Air Staff. In common with the Admiralty, it was felt that the submarine threat had been largely countered by means of ASDIC. The important role for maritime air was therefore felt to be in the detection, tracking and attacking of German surface raiders. On a bureaucratic level, the recent severance of the Fleet Air Arm from RAF control probably did little to encourage cordial relations between the two services.

Despite these very considerable deficiencies, some sensors and weapons at least existed to deal with submarines. The same could not be said for what would now be called wide-area or open-ocean sensors. There was very little chance of detecting, far less doing anything about, submarines between them leaving their bases and their arrival in the vicinity of targets or escorts, unless the submarine was either very unfortunate or else badly handled. The British shore radio direction finding service was initially of poor quality and of little use in helping locate submarines. At this stage, there was no ability to break submarine codes. In any case, during this stage of the campaign most submarines operated singly against independently sailed ships, rather than the later, co-ordinated operations against convoys which made lavish use of radio.

In sum, therefore, all participants were unprepared both in terms of submarines, ships and aircaft; and of ASW equipment. The immediate institution of a convoy system was probably the most important and effective ASW measure taken at the outset.

Although some effort has been expended on establishing initial conditions, it is important to grasp the starting point for the story which developed. In strategic terms, events moved first in the German direction. Not only were they able to deploy more and more submarines into the Atlantic, from 8 per month at the beginning of this period to 32 at the end[7], but once France had fallen in the summer of 1940, they were also able to make use of the Biscay ports. Such a deployment took them out of the strategic "blind alley" and allowed them a relatively easy passage to their targets. There was an added double bonus in that not only were some at least of the French vessels lost to the Allied cause[8], but many of the destroyers that might have been used for convoy were required to be kept close to the United Kingdom to guard against the risk of invasion.

By the onset of the winter of 1940-41, the risk of this had largely passed, freeing ships for ASW tasks: the fate of Operation *Seelöwe* was finally sealed by the German invasion of the USSR in the summer of 1941.

Another strategic theme working on the side of Britain was growing co-operation from the United States of America. The US was technically neutral throughout the period, but took a growing part in the Battle of the Atlantic, if nowhere else. Roosevelt was greatly constrained by a Congress which was not entirely benevolent, a significant amount of neutralist sentiment in the country and by his overriding objective of re-election in the autumn of 1940. Nevertheless, the USA gave more and more facilities to Britain and Canada: the culmination of this was probably the transfer of 50 old destroyers to Britain in the latter half of 1941[9]. It was not so much that these were instantly useful[10], rather that they later allowed substantial reinforcement of convoy escorts, and served as a potent symbol of future co-operation.

At a lower level, not only were more warships, often designed specifically for escort work, being built but their equipment was also being improved. Radar was starting to become fitted reasonably widely, ASDIC was being improved steadily as were methods of delivering weapons to the submarine target.

But it was in the air that perhaps the greatest improvements were being made. New aircraft, with the capability of providing convoy cover to greater ranges were being brought into service. Airborne radar was becoming more widely fitted allowing the detection of surfaced submarines at night or when the aircraft was above cloud, and therefore invisible to the submarine. However, attack at night might still be virtually impossible; it was to require the later development of the Leigh Light to make this feasible.

Growing participation by Canadian, and later American, forces allowed protection to convoys over more and more of their passage. However, the growing numbers of submarines allowed the development of group attacks on convoys. When well co-ordinated and executed, these could result in the overwhelming of inadequate numbers of escorts, and subsequent heavy losses.

An example of this would be convoy HX 126 which in May 1941, eastbound from North America, was intercepted by a line of nine submarines south of Greenland and suffered the loss of nine ships over two days. The convoy only had a light escort at the time of the attack, and this number of sinkings was instrumental in the institution of end-to-end support for future convoys. On the other hand, ten days in March of the same year saw the sinking of no less than three of the most famous U-boat aces, Prien, Kretschmer and Schepke.

It was, however, during this early half of 1941 that the U-boats enjoyed some of their greatest successes, and achieved briefly the efficiency of sinking that they needed to win not just the tonnage war in which they were already engaged, but the one that was to come, an altogether harder proposition. So despite all the Allied advances, submarines had emerged largely ahead in the early period.

THE MIDDLE PART: JANUARY 1942 – MID 1943

The Battle was to take one of its most significant turns at the end of 1941: indeed it could well be argued that the most important event of the whole campaign was the entry into the war of the USA. The obvious way in which this helped was by greatly increasing the number of escorts available for convoy work, and by giving access to more aircraft for ASW. These were essential attributes, but it can be proposed that the most important aspect was the enormous capability of the USA to build merchant ships. Two ways to set this in context are that:

- the building against sinkings balance for the whole war thus far had been brought into net gain by the second half of 1943, little more than a year after America's entry into the war.

- the consequent rate of sinking necessary to stay in balance (i.e. keep the merchant fleets from growing) was only achieved twice during the war, and only once after US entry[11].

Despite these optimistic auspices the period was to start poorly for the Allies, however, with great successes for the U-boats, off the east coast of the USA. These could be attributed not so much to the skill and audacity of the submarines, as to the mistakes in strategy made by the Americans. For reasons which are initially not clear, they did not learn from either 1917 or the more recent British experience: convoy was not begun immediately, and various other sensible and practicable countermeasures were not instituted. Consequently, U-boats enjoyed their second *Gluckliche Zeit* or "Happy time", picking off easily-found targets with virtual impunity.

As a result, not only were a large number of ships disposed of, but the tonnage sunk per submarine deployed per month, was also very high. In economic terms, Dönitz was receiving a very good return in sinkings for his investment of resources. This happened despite the very long (and unproductive) passage times involved. Such passages also tested the fuel endurance of the submarines considerably, and such expedients as single engine running were widely employed and filling drinking water tanks with fuel.

Once on the east coast, targets sailing independently but close to a coast that was often still lit at night, were only too easy to sight, track and despatch. ASW vessels were rarely in the same vicinity and would invariably arrive at the scene of sinkings long after the perpetrator had departed.

Some of the reasons given by the Americans for not starting a convoy system echo similar British reluctance in the First World War: convoy would only concentrate targets; escort numbers were inadequate to allow effective defence and, as in 1917, there was an instinctive judgement made that more "offensive" methods such as patrol groups would gain greater results. Doubtless in early 1941 these beliefs were held as sincerely as they had been in the earlier conflict. But there was a further factor in the form of Admiral Ernest King, Commander in Chief, United States Fleet, later also US Chief of Naval Operations who was not an unqualified admirer of all things British. It is now generally agreed that his views delayed the adoption of various "British" solutions to the problem, such as naval control of shipping and a convoy system. For whatever reasons, the method – or rather lack of it – allowed Dönitz's submarines a very effective period of operations against shipping.

Eventually, however, a system of convoy was instituted and by the middle of 1942 submarine operations were forced either further afield – for instance, to the Caribbean and southern Africa – or back to the main transatlantic convoy routes. Within a year this fighting was to reach its climax and, some would say, its result.

Although the vast war-production of the USA – initially potential, later actual – was to permit a very large build-up not only in merchant vessels, but also in warships, aircraft, equipment and ammunition, two factors constrained its immediate efficacy. One was that a considerable effort had to be devoted not necessarily to securing an immediate victory in the Pacific, but to putting a check on the spread of the Japanese. Although inter-allied conferences quickly established the primacy of the European theatre, the resources devoted to the Pacific were large.

Amongst the equipment, ships and aircraft which began to put in an appearance during this period was the true specialist convoy escort. It mattered little whether this was called a frigate (UK) or destroyer escort (USA); more important were its characteristics of good endurance, reasonable speed, a modicum of comfort in Atlantic conditions, a good fit of sensors and an adequate stock of weapons to allow prolonged prosecution of submarines. The component parts themselves improved in both quality and quantity. Radars became more reliable and widely fitted. The relatively mundane technique of improving illuminants also made the surfaced submarine more vulnerable to gunfire. Their performance against surfaced submarines improved, making the group, night surface attack a riskier proposition against a well defended convoy. Alternatively, the same degree of success against convoys could only be achieved by using more submarines, and the time and effort to coordinate such an attack absorbed a greater number of submarine-days than would have been the case earlier in the war.

Other sensor-weapon combinations rendered the underwater volume much less safe than it had been. Ships no longer needed to overrun their targets to attack, thus losing ASDIC (or sonar to the Americans) contact. Weapons could be projected for greater distances in a more flexible array of directions using simple depth charge mortars, Hedgehog and later more sophisticated throwers. The acoustic homing ASW torpedo was also about to be deployed.

Ships working in teams of two or more were able to bring increasing pressure to bear on a single submarine. Sinking a submarine involves a complex equation of factors, of which one of the most important is time: more lavish provision of escorts to convoys allowed the luxury of being able to carry on the prosecution for longer. If the submarine was not sunk, or even rendered incapable of continuing its patrol, it might well be held long enough in one position to allow the convoy to move far enough away to obviate the risk of further attack from that submarine.

By the end of the period, the relative abundance of ASW ships permitted the deployment not only of adequate close escorts, but also the formation of separate support groups, which could be used either to reinforce convoys which were particularly threatened (always provided that there was sufficient warning of that risk), or for other task such as the extirpation of supply submarines. Some of these groups gained considerable expertise, and not a little renown.

But it can be argued that the greatest advances in ASW were made in this period not on the surface, but in the air. Here an enormous expansion was much in evidence. In Coastal Command the number of aircraft had risen from a figure of well under 200 at the outbreak of war to about 450 by the middle of 1943. More importantly, the quality of aircraft had improved immensely. Coastal Command had started the war with very few aircraft, and of these only two types, the Hudson and Sunderland, even approached any form of ASW capability. The worst limitation of other aircraft was lack of range, although as adduced earlier, equipment was of a rudimentary nature.

However, any form of aircraft in the vicinity of a submarine tends to have a deterrent effect, and much of the period from the outbreak of war to the middle of 1943 concerned bringing convoys not only under surface escort, but also air cover. Surface escorts excelled in providing close protection to shipping and during long prosecutions of submarines; aircraft could search large areas and provide rapid reaction to detections of submarines still some way from convoys. The two types of ASW unit thus possess mutually reinforcing characteristics and it is a mistake to ever see them as being in competition for some mythical "best ASW buy". The extension of air cover was attained by three means:

- Basing aircraft in more places along the routes, especially in the western (the USA and Canada) and Central Atlantic (Iceland and the Azores).

- The introduction of longer range aircraft, especially of those of American provenance.

- Escort aircraft carriers.

Little needs to be said about basing, a relatively straightforward story, although perhaps plots operating from Iceland in the middle of winter might feel otherwise. The excellent Sunderland continued to rise in numbers and was joined by the smaller but also long-legged Catalina. A later arrival was the Liberator, originally conceived as a land bomber. This brought the very latest aircraft technology to the maritime war, and was to be used to great effect by its crews. The aircraft could spend some three hours on patrol at a range of 1,000 miles from base, was fitted with radar and carried a variety of weapons from cannon for attacking surfaced submarines to depth charges for the submerging target. The provision of such VLR aircraft was, however, a matter of some disputes as the same production could be devoted to bombers: it is perhaps telling that no British true VLR aircraft went into service.

But other aircraft were also able to pay a part, both closer to the Western approaches and in such areas as the Bay of Biscay. By the middle of 1943 the practice of attacking U-boats on surface transit outbound from the French bases, such as La Pallice and Brest, through the Bay of Biscay, became particularly successful. The effectiveness of such operations has been a matter of some controversy[12], but there is little doubt that the ability to influence the conduct of enemy operations, coupled with the probable slowing of deployment to operational areas and, above all, the early-application of pressure on the crew did little to increase the operational efficiency of the submarines.

The air gap was also catered for by the introduction of escort aircraft carriers. These vessels, scaled down versions of their larger and more famous sisters, often utilised the hulls of merchant vessels and were sometimes limited to carrying ASW aircraft only. Although such aeroplanes were often not at the forefront of design, they nevertheless provided airborne eyes: moreover, several submariners had cause to regret the appearance of a rocket-firing or depth charge carrying Swordfish.

The practical application of such aircraft and their weapons to the ASW battle was very much enhanced by the use of operational research techniques. This paper is not the place to elaborate on this topic, but it is important to note that although OR was also used in surface ASW, its widest usage was probably in ASW air matters. It is sufficient to note that it enhanced operations by addressing such ground-borne subjects as maintenance and patrol scheduling; through navigational techniques; to search and attack tactics.

The German efforts in the field of maritime air stand in sharp contrast to the Allied achievement. Their objectives were somewhat different, being to attack shipping and ocean reconnaissance in support of submarines. It is perhaps helpful to dispose of the attack role first. When these operations were undertaken, the Germans often enjoyed success, notwithstanding the fact that only a limited number of aircraft types had the range and navigational capability to operate effectively over water. Their numbers, largely of Condor, and the relatively infrequency of such operations meant, however, that aircraft added only a marginal increment to the submarine totals in the tonnage war. Effective countermeasures also came to be deployed at sea to this threat with the advent of CAM ships* and eventually the escort carrier.

Such relative success compares well, nevertheless, to the German record in ocean reconnaissance by aircraft. It was not that the Navy in general, and Dönitz in particular, did not recognise its value. There were also aircraft suitable for the task; again the Condor served well. It is important to understand the value of reconnaissance. It is, of course, possible for submarines unaided to find convoys – they did this frequently. However, even a string of submarines drawn up across the likely path of a convoy is a poor and very inefficient way in which to search for shipping. The convoy itself may occupy several square miles, and may be visible for some twenty miles beyond that, but it is sailing in a very large ocean; the fin of a submarine only a few feet above sea-level is poor place from which to see thousands of square miles of water. The aircraft, by comparison, is good at searching large areas. To exploit the aircraft's characteristics best, a degree of continuity or endurance is required to allow closure of submarines and take some account of mutual navigational errors, and the number of aircraft was generally inadequate for that task.

* See Addendum

But these largely technical points were as nothing to the bureaucratic impasse. Goering, in charge of the *Luftwaffe* did not approve of operations in support of the *Kriegsmarine* and also stood in the way of the German Navy having its own aircraft. Thus maritime reconnaissance was sporadic, lacked the expertise that comes with constant practice, and thus largely ineffective. From a German viewpoint, this was a most significant defect in their conduct of the Battle. From time to time, some British naval historians, have voiced complaint about the standard of co-operation between the RAF and Royal Navy, usually citing difficulties over the supply of VLR aircraft, against the competing priority of the bomber. Even if this is accepted as being true, it could be said with some confidence, that Dönitz would have dearly loved to have had such problems.

A last point on improvements in the Allies' position concerns the ability to find submarines over wide sea areas. This desiderata was becoming regularly attainable by means of two techniques of SIGINT: decryption and HF DF. Both exploited the necessity for extensive communication by submarines involved in the preliminaries to group attacks. Decryption had involved widespread efforts by the British and others throughout the war. 1941 had seen some successes on U-boat codes, but these had been frustrated by the introduction of a further layer of complication in the code system. This was overcome by late in 1942, and was to play an important part in ASW from then on.

A further reaction to the abundant use of HF radio by the submarines was the development and fitting of HF DF to escorts. This enabled the tactical exploitation of submarine transmissions. In the beginning, it was not always possible to prosecute on the basis of all such information, because of the paucity of escorting forces. Latterly, however, as the growing number of escorts permitted the formation of support groups additional to the close convoy escort, the ability to follow up DF bearings was improved. The ever growing density of air support was also important in this respect. These tactics did not always result in the sinking of U-boats, but they did little to improve the submarines' prosecution of the convoys.

Lest it should be considered that SIGINT was a one-sided activity it is worth considering that the German xB-Dienst was able to penetrate British convoy codes, particularly in the earlier part of the war[13]. This was eventually discovered by the British and remedial measures taken. The same could not be said of the

Germans, but it is worth remembering R V Jones dictum that in intelligence the negative case which is that the enemy does not have a particular capability is always the most difficult to prove[14].

It is now helpful to look very briefly at two important actions which took place in 1943. In March of that year no less than four groups totalling 45 submarines were cued by xB-Dienst decrypts against two eastbound convoys in the "air gap" south of Iceland. These two convoys, HX 229 and SC 122, had an understrength escort and what was described by Hessler as the "Biggest Convoy Operation of the War" ensued. Over the next four days, more than twenty merchant vessels were sunk and others damaged for the loss of a single submarine[15]. By May, however, the situation had changed completely and in that month no less than 41 submarines were lost. This was also one of the most successful periods for the Bay offensive, which claimed some seven victims, but the majority of the losses were in the vicinity of convoys, sunk by either surface escorts or aircraft.

In sum, therefore, the U-boats started the period on the high note of the Second *Gluckliche Zeit,* but ended by being forced to retreat from the Atlantic. This had been brought about not by dint of any single dramatic breakthrough in strategy or technology by the Allies, but by the remorseless build-up in escort vessels, aircraft and merchant ships coupled with improved weapons, techniques and supporting activities. In short, an integrated ASW system – although no one at the time would have used such a term – had succeeded, at least for the time being in defeating an extensive, professional and determined submarine assault on shipping.

THE END: MID 1943-MAY 1945

It might seem that the Battle was over by the middle of 1943; but this would be to make a judgement in hindsight. Dönitz's U-boats certainly left the open Atlantic, never again to repeat the performance of the earlier years, despite several attempts. The tactics of group attack were abandoned to be replaced by the operations of independent submarines. These were often situated in coastal waters, increasing the chances of finding targets, but also making the task of the ASW forces easier to some extent. There nevertheless remained considerable concern that the U-boat threat could again revive to pose a significant threat to the shipping necessary to sustain the forthcoming European offensive[16].

Such a concern was not misplaced because there were several technical developments which might have proved a considerable nuisance, if not actually generating a critical threat to supplies. The basic design of submarine had advanced hardly at all from 1939 until the middle of 1943. The Type VIIs and IXs formed the backbone of the oceangoing fleet. They were improved in detail, but essentially the same in 1943 as four years earlier. The main limitations of such boats were their slow underwater speed and poor endurance, and these drawbacks were well known. The route to improvement lay through two means: improving the hydrodynamic performance of the hull and creating a high performance, air independent propulsion system. During the course of the war, the first was attained, but the second largely eluded solution.

The earliest, yet most-radical, of these developments was the Walter boat, a submarine of extremely high underwater performance. This was achieved by means of a very much improved hull form and a revolutionary power plant, which utilised a turbine driven by potent but very unstable chemicals such as hydrogen peroxide. Although demonstrated as early as 1940, the design never went into operational service. Some of the Walter boat's characteristics were perpetuated in the Electroboats.

These were started much later and merged the hydrodynamic features of the Walter submarines with a modified but essentially conventional diesel-electric power plant. The main improvement in the machinery was a battery of very much higher capacity. This, in tactical terms, allowed the possibility of relatively sustained, underwater high speed evasion after attack thus negating the various forms of 'flaming datum' ASW searches and counter attacks. These techniques found expression in the Type XXI, a 2,100 ton submarine and the Type XXIII, a 250 ton boat. Neither of these were available in time to have any significant influence on the course of the war, although both types were deployed operationally. The potential of these submarines was nevertheless very considerable, and knowledge of their development and production spurred Allied efforts to prevent as many as possible of these going to sea. For many years bomber effort had been directed against U-boat bases and production facilities, but lack of the necessary accuracy had rendered such attacks largely ineffective: by now, however, it proved possible to disrupt the deployment of Types XXI and XXIII to a considerable extent.

A further development was simple, most widely used and possibly the most significant. The Schnorkel had first been used in modern times by the Royal Netherlands Navy, whose submarines fitted with the device were captured by the Germans in 1940. They had not immediately appreciated the significance of the equipment but in 1943, as it became more and more difficult to operate submarines, the idea was revived. The Schnorkel was to take the diesel electric submarine as close to being a true submarine as possible but in submarine warfare terms it offered few real advantages to the Germans. Certainly it made radar detection more difficult and thus negated much of the effectiveness of aircraft as sinkers of submarines but, in the views of one commentator it "...only provided the difference between death and meagre survival." It also created other problems, limiting speed in pursuit of a convoy and making living conditions, already poor, near-nigh intolerable. A more significant problem, apparently not taken account of, was the extreme limitation of the submarine's visual horizon. In the general absence of effective external targeting, it is unlikely that boats limited to a periscope's optical limits would have been very successful at finding convoys. The Schnorkel boats that were deployed were often used in the target rich coastal waters around the United Kingdom, where such a limitation was of little account. It must therefore be considered that the Schnorkel enhanced survivability to the considerable detriment of anti-shipping capability.

Detailed improvements to the submarines resulted in improved ability, to detect both air- and shipborne radar, but there were many false steps along the way brought about by both by technical difficulty and gross misappreciatations of intelligence. By the time that such a device became reliable, it could only serve as a survival aid, rather than enhancing operational performance. For much of the war, the submarines had no weapon specifically designed for use against escorts. However, in September 1943 the U-boats first made use of an anti-escort homing acoustic torpedo, the Zaunkönig, which enjoyed some initial success. The Germans overestimated its effects, and countermeasures – both tactical and material – were very quickly devised and implemented. It is idle but fascinating to speculate on the effect of a very much earlier introduction of Zaunkönig during the period of the most critical shortages of escorts.

Various attempts were made by the submarine command to deal with the problem of aircraft, usually by means of increasing the calibre and number of guns. There were instances in which submarines downed aircraft, but not sufficiently often to encourage the tactic of staying on the surface to fight it out. in any case, the latter Allied preponderance, both in the air and on the surface allowed the development of tactics to counter "flak traps".

On the Allied side, most of the major innovations had already been set in train by the end of 1943. The main improvements were qualitative and, above all, in quantity. The anti-submarine homing torpedo, otherwise dignified by the cover name of the Mark 24 mine was an example of technological advance. This was used successfully against submarines using sufficient speed for their propellers to cavitate[17]. A parallel development was that of sonobuoys, allowing a submerged submarine to be detected by an aircraft for the first time. Such devices were not ineffective, but their principal value lay in the future, rather than being significant factors in the Battle of the Atlantic.

One operation which demonstrated the supremacy of the Allies, together with their ability to produce novel plans suited to particular situations was the ASW protection of the forces for the invasion of Normandy. Here, the aim was to prevent the penetration of U-boats to areas where they could attack the large amount of shipping necessary for the operation during its passage to France. Several escort groups were used on the surface, together with a large number of aircraft, flying in skilfully designed patrol patterns such that it would be very difficult indeed for a submarine to make any use of the surface whatsoever. Although submarines were held back until it became plain that the Allied operation was, in fact, a full offensive and not just a strategic feint, it was only some of these, that is those fitted with Schnorkel, which succeeded in reaching the invasion area. Despite this several submarines were sunk in exchange for rather fewer merchant sinkings.

It may be remembered that Dönitz was by now justifying the submarine campaign with the rationale that no matter how many submarines were sunk, and how few merchant ships, the battle was worth fighting because of the vast resources devoted to ASW by the Allies. As it went, this argument was acceptable, but it ignored the ability and will of the Allies to pay this price. The world's largest ever ASW battle was being fought at the same time as a large bombing campaign; as ground forces were steadily reoccupying Europe supported by huge tactical air forces, as the largest known army was advancing from the east on Berlin, and whilst the Japanese were being steadily rolled back across the Pacific. The Allies were hardly technologically backward, but as was noted in a remark usually attributed to Stalin, "Quantity has a quality all of its own."

To return to the Atlantic, perhaps the last twenty four months can best be summed up by one statistical observation. In Professor Rohwer's book *Axis Submarine Successes,* the first 45 months of war generate nearly 170 pages of tabular accounts of submarine attacks: the latter 24 months less than 30.

NOTES

1. The exact number is a matter of some doubt.
2. Hitler's table-talk is notable for the <u>lack</u> of comment on maritime matters, even the efforts of the U-boats.
3. Rohwer (1); p.1 notes the falsification of the submarine's war diary.
4. He produces a persuasive rationale for this figure in his memoirs; Dönitz, pp37–41.
5. Frigates and corvettes were not yet available in appreciable numbers.
6. The first submarine kill attributed to surface vessel radar did not take place until March 1941. Barley and Waters; p68.
7. Averaged on the basis of six month calendar periods.
8. Either directly by falling into German hands, or by internment.
9. Both Roosevelt and Churchill played an important personal part in this transaction. See Kimball 1, Documents C-17x and R-8x.
10. They needed extensive conversion for ASW work. Kimball 1; C-53X/A.
11. Calculated in terms of sinking, rate attained per submarine deployed compounded by the number actually deployed.
12. Barley and Waters; p229 is generally dismissive of the Bay campaign, but notes that its use of aircraft which did not have the range to be of use in the broad Atlantic meant that there was no significant opportunity lost thereby.
13. Some care must be taken with attributing significance to SIGINT. Roskill considered that decrypted intelligence was of critical importance to the Germans *only* between 1942 and 1944. Roskill Papers 4/42. Similar caution might also apply to ULTRA.
14. Jones; P576.
15. Middlebrook and Rohwer(2) write complimentary accounts. The former scores on personal details; the latter on analysis. Rohwer probably passes the *Desert Island Discs* test.
16. This subject is discussed at some length in Marc Milner: "The Dawn of Modern Anti-Submarine Warfare" *RUSI Journal,* Spring 1989; and subsequent correspondence in the Autumn and Winter editions of the same year.
17. A state of enhanced noise made at certain speeds and depths.

6. Intelligence

Mr. Edward Thomas

Almost exactly 50 years ago, in September 1941, I was one of the first to board a virtually intact U-boat. U-570 had surrendered to a Hudson of 269 Squadron, Coastal Command, and was beached at a desolate spot on the south coast of Iceland. It was on her engines that I first saw the magic letters "BMW". Earlier that year, as naval intelligence officer in Iceland, I had been interrogating survivors of the many merchant ships sunk in the, at first, highly successful offensive launched by Dönitz, C in C U-boats, in March 1941. I had spent many hours trying to analyse the numbers and tactics of the U-boats making the attacks, but could have spared my pains for within a few months I was at Bletchley Park discovering that there was not much they, and the Admiralty's Submarine Tracking Room, did not know about the U-boats.

My first job there was to edit and translate, at breakneck speed, decrypts of signals passing between Dönitz and his boats at sea. Bletchley had started to break the daily-changing Home Waters settings of the German Navy's ENIGMA cypher in the spring of 1941 which, at the time, carried 95% of its radio message traffic, including that of the U-boats. From March to May it had been read haltingly and often retrospectively; but from the beginning of June it was broken currently and mostly soon enough to be used operationally. Its yield, and that of other enemy highgrade cyphers, became known as ULTRA Other intelligence sources – notably air patrols, the RAF's indispensable photo reconnaissance (PR), HF/DF, POW interrogation, captured documents and equipment – contributed to the Battle of the Atlantic, their value being greatly enhanced when interpreted against the background of ULTRA which, though of course absolutely reliable, was incomplete in many respects. But today I shall have to concentrate on ULTRA, and that only in the broadest outline. Nor will there be time to discuss the anti-shipping activities of the German Navy's surface raiders or the German Air Force (GAF). In any case these declined, by coincidence, at about the time ULTRA came on stream.

It was most fortunate that this breakthrough coincided with Dönitz's spring offensive. Up till then very little had been learned about the two dozen or so U-boats at sea which, against our then rudimentary defences, had had things pretty much their own way. Their offensive had been launched in the confidence that their former high rate of merchant ship sinkings could be not only maintained but decisively increased as more U-boats arrived on the scene. In this way Dönitz hoped to knock out Britain while the German armies disposed of Russia and before help from the United States could reach significant proportions. A two-front war would thus be avoided. In Whitehall, as the offensive got under way, the outlook was bleak. Unless sinkings could be reduced Britain would be crippled before new merchant ships could be built fast enough to maintain imports at the level needed for Britain's survival.

At this point ULTRA stepped in. It provided two sorts of intelligence. Firstly, that for immediate operational use. The U-boats were now employing wolf-pack tactics against the vital North Atlantic convoys. These tactics called for the transmission by boats of sighting reports and homing signals so that other boats could be ordered to concentrate and attack from the surface by night in areas out of range of Coastal Command. Convoys were, at this time, virtually defenceless against these tactics. But for their success all depended on tightly centralised control by U-boat Command and the transmission of a stream of tactical orders, patrol instructions, situation reports and exhortations. This made them vulnerable to ULTRA and, as we shall hear later, to HF/DF – as well as to ASV. Secondly ULTRA provided, in huge quantity, less immediate but equally valuable background information such as U-boat 'kills' particularly valuable in the case of Mk 24 mine attacks the rate of commissioning (the rate of construction coming from PR), exit and approach routes from and to bases, and the frequency of patrols. It also revealed operational characteristics such as the speed, diving depths, endurance, armament, signals and radar equipment of the different types of U-boat, and the current operational state of boats at sea.

Despite ULTRA, merchant ship sinkings remained high in June 1941. This was partly because of difficulties, constantly to recur, in interpreting the disguised grid references for U-boat positions in the decrypts, and partly because U-boats were now sent for the first time to West African waters. Here the defences were unprepared and great toll was taken of ships sailing independently. These U-boats had to return at the end of June since they were unable to refuel, the tankers sent into the Atlantic to supply them (and the BISMARCK) having been sunk, nearly all with the aid of ULTRA. When the U-boats returned to this area in September they achieved little since convoys had now been instituted and could now be routed clear of danger by means of ULTRA. This ended German attempts to maintain U-boats in distant waters through the help of surface supply ships.

The North Atlantic saw an even more important, if not dramatic, decline in sinkings from the end of June. This was partly because steps had been taken to reduce the number of independents, but mainly because ULTRA-directed evasive routeing – that is, steering convoys clear of known U-boat patrol lines (grid reference difficulties now having been temporarily solved) - could now be practised on a large scale. By the summer of 1941 Coastal Command had driven the U-boats westward beyond the range of air patrols. But this gave more scope for evasive routeing which at once brought about a steep fall in the number of convoy attacks . Sinkings dropped from 300,000 tons in May and June to 100,000 in July and August. Mystified, Dönitz switched his boats back and forth in a mostly vain effort to find convoys. He had occasional successes from sightings by U-boats on passage of whose position ULTRA was unaware. Others were scored against Gibraltar convoys where the U-boats benefited from GAF recce and where there was less scope for evasive routeing. In late summer they were moved nearer the UK where, their positions being known, they were effectively harried by Coastal. Heartened by this, and by the drop in sinkings, it was proposed that Coastal's few VLR Liberators be switched to Bomber Command. Fortunately, in the light of what was to come, this was resisted.

In September sinkings rose again, mainly because of renewed grid reference difficulties. But by October these had been overcome; evasive routeing could again be practised and sinkings again declined, despite the fact that the number of U-boats known to be at sea – now 80 – was double that at the start of the offensive. In November sinkings dropped to 62,000 tons, the lowest for 18 months. At this point many boats were diverted to the Arctic and Mediterranean while the rest were mostly concentrated off Gibraltar, to which area Coastal's patrols were at once directed. The offensive against the trans-Atlantic routes was, for the time being, virtually abandoned.

Some historians see the end of 1941, despite the horrors to come, as the turning point in the Battle of the Atlantic, the 300 ships calculated as having been saved by evasive routeing not only defeating Dönitz's offensive but also providing a cushion against the heavy losses yet to come. The second half of 1941 also provided something of a breathing space in which the Allies could forge ahead with the development of anti-submarine weapons and tactics, and lay the foundations for the later surge in merchant ship building which was to ensure victory. ULTRA was to share later triumphs with the operational forces. But for this one it was alone responsible.

At the beginning of 1942 the Germans responded to the suspicions aroused by their setbacks of 1941 and the sinking of their supply ships. They suspected ENIGMA compromise, but were assured it must be treachery or the opportunities for espionage arising from internal insecurity. In February they introduced a new and more complex form of ENIGMA cypher solely for use with U-boats at sea, except for those in the Arctic and Mediterranean, and tightened up security all round. Called TRITON by the Germans, this new ENIGMA defeated Bletchley for ten months and deprived the Allies – for the Americans had been admitted to the ULTRA secret well before Pearl Harbor and had been taking an active part in the Atlantic battle – of their special knowledge of U-boat operations. Fortunately the original Home Waters settings of the ENIGMA could still be broken and continued to provide useful background information such as the arrival and departure of U-boats at their bases, and the rate of commissions. Furthermore, the Allies had by then built up a sound knowledge of U-boat operational practice and organisation – and even of Dönitz's habits of mind. But as regards convoy defence they were blind. Greater reliance had now to be placed on HF/DF and ever-improving air patrols. But they were a poor substitute for ULTRA. The Bletchley black-out concealed, amongst other things, the renewed successes of the German cypher-breakers the xB-Dienst (of which more later) - and the introduction of supply U-boats of new type which almost doubled the effectiveness of the ever increasing number of U-boats in the Atlantic and enabled them to operate in fruitful distant waters. The first supply U-boat to be sunk was one of Coastal's victims in the second half of 1942 all achieved without help from ULTRA.

For the first six months of 1942 U-boat activity was concentrated off the coasts of north America. Here there was great carnage. Merchant ship sinkings rose from 50,000 tons in December 1941 to unprecedented half-million in March. ULTRA would have been of little use here, even if it had been available, for the Atlantic was virtually deserted and the boats in American coastal waters operated independently of control from Germany. Only their numbers were known, never their whereabouts – at least, not from ULTRA. Not until mid-1942, with the belated American introduction of convoy and the establishment of a Tracking Room in Washington DC (in close daily touch with London and Ottawa), did US defences improve sufficiently for Dönitz to decide to send some of his boats to even more distant waters, and to return the bulk of them to the Atlantic convoy routes. The total of operational boats had now risen, as ULTRA revealed, from 100 in January 1942 to 150.

From August 1942 the U-boats inflicted ever more serious losses in the Atlantic. Convoys were occasionally diverted on the strength of air sightings and HF/DF. But without TRITON Admiralty was unable to steer them clear of the ever-lengthening patrol lines. Furthermore, the U-boats were now obtaining valuable help from their own cypher-breakers – the xB-Dienst – in finding targets. Up to August 1940 this remarkable service had had much success against the Royal Navy's general cypher. But during most of 1941 they went blind, and it was largely this that prevented them from twigging the connection between evasive routeing and ENIGMA compromise. Fortunately for us, it also provided the Germans with a part excuse for their own failures in 1941. In the summer of 1941 the Royal Navy intoduced a new cypher often called the "Convoy Cypher" - for carrying the bulk of Atlantic convoy message traffic between the Allies. This the xB-Dienst broke in February 1942 – by sad coincidence also the month when Bletchley lost its grip on the U-boat traffic. The Convoy Cypher was of no great use to the U-boats during the campaign in US coastal waters: but from August 1942 it contributed much to their great and growing successes against the Atlantic convoys.

But serious as these were they were exceeded by the losses inflicted in the South Atlantic and Indian Ocean. Here the U-boats operated as lone wolves and took great toll of ships sailing independently, convoy and evasive routeing being largely impracticable in those remote areas. Even if it had been available ULTRA would have been of little use in this situation. The upshot was that, despite the growing number of Allied surface and air escorts, total merchant ships losses so mounted that in November 1942 they reached an all-time record of 700,000 tons. For the Germans continuation of such success seemed their only hope of pulling through the war, for Stalingrad was now putting paid to any hope of defeating Russia. As for Britain the optimism of 12 months earlier now vanished. With Allied shipping under the greatest possible strain the outlook was bleak in the extreme. Unless the rate of loss could be reduced there seemed no prospect that the construction of new merchant tonnage could outstrip sinkings. In December 1942 the Admiralty appealed desperately to Bletchley who, they said, could alone save the situation.

By a further amazing coincidence it was in that very month that papers recovered from a U-boat sinking off Port Said enabled Bletchley at last to break into TRITON. In December it revealed that Dönitz, now with nearly 50 boats in the North Atlantic, was preparing to launch a big offensive in the Greenland Gap. Decrypts came less regularly than in 1941; but even so Dönitz was frustrated in January and most of February 1943. Sinkings dropped and many valuable convoys were saved by evasive routeing. Another stroke of fortune was that, during these months, the xB-Dienst temporarily lost its ability to read the Convoy Cypher. This prevented them from detecting why circumstances had changed. But they recovered it towards the end of February; and in March Bletchley lost its grip on TRITON for nearly a fortnight.

These factors, and wolf-packs of unprecedented size, made March the worst month ever for convoy sinkings, and the fifth worst month of all. Atlantic convoys, now carrying US forces to Europe, were running at twice their previous rate and the xB-Dienst had little difficulty in picking them out while Bletchley was halting or silent. The Admiralty feared that, with U-boats saturating the North Atlantic, the days of evasive routeing – and, indeed, of the very convoy system were numbered. Never, they said, had Britain's lifeline come so near to being severed.

In April Bletchley made a partial recovery. Evasive routeing sometimes succeeded; but was as often frustrated by xB-Dienst counter-action. However, it was Allied operational capabilities that now turned the tide. By the end of March Coastal's slowly growing force of VR Liberators and aircraft from the first escort carrier, were closing the Greenland Gap and forcing U-boat shadowers to submerge. Improved A/S weapons and tactics now made themselves felt. Shipborne HF/DF now maximised its exploitation of the radio transmissions of the crowded U-boats, often succeeding in steering convoys clear of danger and helping air and surface escorts to find, and kill, U-boats. Above all centimetric radar, now installed in surface escorts and – as ASV III – in aircraft was turning them into deadly U-boat killers.

These developments, together with the skill and courage of the attackers, were responsible – as ULTRA showed – for the sinking of 56 U-boats in the three months to the end of May compared with the 51 that left port, for the first time a net decrease in their operational number. Signs of flagging morale now appeared in the TRITON decrypts along with references to the U-boats' growing fear of air attack and the speed with which surface escorts followed up air sightings. By 19 April, as the decrypts showed, Dönitz was conceding that Allied air was frustrating pack attack. And on 25 May he withdrew his boats to the central Atlantic beyond the reach of Allied air. And at about this time statistics showed that new merchant ship construction was beginning to overtake sinkings.

During the melée each side learned that the other was somehow learning of the movements and whereabouts of his forces. The Allies, now convinced of the compromise of the Convoy Cypher, immediately brought a new one into force, and from June 1943 onwards the Germans were denied virtually all intelligence of Allied shipping movements, for their part attributing the Allies' excellent intelligence to their miraculous detection devices.

If ULTRA played second fiddle operationally during these climactic months, its background information was now being widely used, suitably disguised, to inform manuals of A/S warfare, convoy conferences, post mortems, and briefings at every level in the RAF and Navy. We may guess that this helped to boost the competence and confidence with which the battle was fought. John Terraine, reflecting on "the awesome effectiveness of anti-U-boat warfare by mid-1943" writes that "operational intelligence was evidently central to this: when it was not available, or was incomplete, responsible commanders felt crippled".

From the end of July 1943 Bletchley and its American counterpart broke TRITON regularly till almost the end of the war with only very rare delays. Its recovery was demonstrated when, with its help, American escort carriers and Coastal Command between them proceeded to sink, as well as numerous U-boats, virtually the entire fleet of supply U-boats. This reduced to negligible proportions the campaign in distant waters, by which

Dönitz now set great store, and greatly diminished the effectiveness of those in the central Atlantic. Coastal's contribution to this was incidental to its famous offensive of the summer of 1943 over the Bay of Biscay and the northern U-boat exits. This was made possible by the wholesale withdrawal of aircraft from the North Atlantic, now shown by ULTRA to be free of danger, and was guided in its day-to-day patrols and offensive sweeps largely, though not exclusively, by ULTRA. This gave warning of Dönitz's frequently changed tactics and counter-measures, and often of the movements of the boats themselves. Between May and August almost 30 boats were sunk, including half the fleet of supply U-boats.

In September 1943 Dönitz had one last shot at a North Atlantic offensive. Great preparations were made to ensure secrecy and surprise. These were disclosed by ULTRA; but because of renewed grid reference difficulties the position of the first attack was miscalculated by 100 miles. Consequently the U-boats achieved a measure of surprise and some success with the new acoustic torpedo. Within two months, however, a combination of evasive routeing and vigorous action by air and surface escorts forced Dönitz to abandon pack attacks for good and again to withdraw all but a few boats from the North Ailantic where they continued for months – until D-Day, in fact – to hunt for convoys with negligible success. A strong force was sent to operate against the Gibraltar convoys and during the ensuing months many battles were fought in Iberian waters and the south-western approaches. But here, frustrated by ULTRA-directed air patrols, support groups and evasive routeing, they achieved little and took heavy casualties. From January to March 1944 three merchant ships were sunk out of 3,360 convoyed; and in the whole of 1944 36 were sunk compared with the 121 sunk in November 1942. Air was the major factor in this; and by 1944, as ULTRA revealed, the U-boats were reporting the air situation in the central Atlantic to be more horrific even than Biscay. This was the background to the successful transport of US forces to the UK which made it possible to launch the Normandy landings on time.

Enemy expectation of an invasion of Europe brought about large scale redisposition of the U-boat fleet. The chief reason for its failure to interfere with OVERLORD was the sheer weight of Allied precautionary air and surface patrols planned on the basis of ULTRA. Three months after D-Day ULTRA detected the move to Norway of what was left of the Biscay-based boats. They suffered no losses during their slow progress through heavily patrolled waters because of their ability to move entirely submerged by using the new Schnorkel, or breathing tube. But the Germans went further than that. In the spring of 1944 PR had detected the construction, at an unprecedented rate, of two entirely novel types of U-boat, one evidently ocean-going, and the other of shorter range. This development was the outcome of the Germans' conclusion, after their experiences of 1943, that the older types of boat were no longer viable. Decrypts of Japanese messages from Berlin to Tokyo told us all about the new types. They were being constructed at high speed from components prefabricated all over Germany so as to escape bombing, and these were being brought overland to three shipyards for assembly The decrypts revealed that they were designed to evade Allied A/S measures, having high underwater speed and the ability to cruise entirely submerged with Schnorkel. The new ocean-going boat, called Type XXI, was to be equipped with a formidable array of new attack weapons and detecting devices. The decrypts also revealed that Dönitz intended to build sufficient to re-open the Atlantic battle from bomb-proof shelters in Norway and north Germany in the autumn of 1944, also using old types fitted with Schnorkel. It was mainly because Hitler pinned such high hopes on the new types and on other technical innovations, such as rockets, guided missiles and jet aircraft, that he issued his notorious "no retreat" orders to all and sundry.

Such an offensive would have been highly dangerous. During the autumn of 1944 the older Schnorkel boats were packed round the coasts of Britain where they lay submerged near the intensively used shipping lanes. After some early and unpleasant merchant ship sinkings the threat was taken very seriously indeed. ULTRA revealed their presence but not their precise locations. All Britain's A/S resources had to be mustered to counter them, some being recalled from overseas, while the departure for the Far East of 300 escorts was cancelled. By this means the threat was kept down. But there would have been precious few escorts to spare to deal with a simultaneous Atlantic offensive. Coastal was to find Schnorkel almost totally immune to radar or visual detection.

To make matters worse the amount of U-boat radio traffic now declined drastically. Being submerged the boats transmitted rarely or not at all. They operated independently on orders mostly given before they sailed. Furthermore, the U-boat command now introduced a system of single-boat ENIGMA settings, virtually the equivalent of the one-time pad. This was increasingly distributed from November 1944 and proved virtually unbreakable. Had the Type XXI offensive been launched signals to them would have been made in this new ENIGMA.

What is more, signals from sea would have been made in a newly devised system of very high-speed, off-frequency transmission. Interception and DF would have presented very great difficulties.

What frustrated the Type XXI offensive was, firstly, unexpected teething troubles; and, secondly, Bomber Command. Its attacks on Germany's land communications, especially canals, delayed the movement of pre-fabricated components: its bombing of shipyards delayed assembly: and its ULTRA-directed mining of the Baltic made trials, training and working-up next to impossible. Dönitz had hoped to build 238 by February 1945. By December 1944 ULTRA showed that 15 per month were being commissioned. But the Japanese decrypts revealed the difficulties they were encountering and the regular postponement of the planned offensive. In the event 120 were completed by May 1945. Only one ever sailed, and that on the eve of Germany's capitulation. It achieved nothing. But the last minute successes of the shorter range boat of the new type showed what might have been achieved had the war continued.

To conclude I will quote a further calculation also made by a historian. This was that ULTRA's contribution to winning the Battle of the Atlantic, to say nothing of other campaigns, shortened the war by at least two years. That victory enabled OVERLORD to be launched on time. Any postponement would have had most awkward consequences. Some speculate that the first atomic bomb might have fallen on Hamburg – or Berlin.

7. Development of Equipment and Techniques

Dr. Alfred Price

My part of today's proceedings is to give an outline of the development of equipment and techniques in Coastal Command during the Second World War. To illustrate the tremendous advances made during that period I should like to draw your attention to a couple of incidents, one at the beginning of the war and one almost at the end.

On 5 September 1939, two days after the outbreak of war, an Anson of No 233 Squadron on a daylight patrol off the east coast of Scotland surprised a submarine on the surface. It descended to low altitude to deliver its attack, and as the boat was in the process of crash-diving the pilot released two 100 pound anti-submarine bombs. These weapons were fitted with a double-action fuse, designed to give instantaneous detonation if the weapon struck the submarine on the surface, or detonation after a short delay if the weapon struck the water. Due to the low altitude release, the bombs struck the sea at a shallow angle and bounced back into the air like a couple of flat stones. The force of the impact with the sea initiated their time fuses, however, and after a short delay both the bombs detonated in the air. Several bomb splinters struck the Anson and punctured her fuel tanks. Streaming petrol, the aircraft ran out of fuel short of the coast and the pilot was forced to ditch. The crew took to their dinghy and were rescued soon afterwards.

That was not the end of the incident, however. It later transpired that the submarine was a 'friendly' boat, HMS SEAHORSE. She suffered no damage from the bombs, but during her hasty dive she descended too steeply and struck the sea bed. The boat suffered damage and had to return to port for repairs.

The second incident I wish to describe took place on 20 March 1945, about six weeks before the end of the war against Germany. Acting on ULTRA information, a Liberator of No 86 Squadron was patrolling an area off the Orkneys at night. The radar operator picked up a suspicious contact three miles away and the pilot ran in to investigate, but at a range of half a mile the contact merged into the sea returns and disappeared. The aircraft lookouts saw nothing. The radar operator suspected that the contact he had seen was a schnorkel, however, so the crew spent the next 20 minutes laying out a pattern of five passive sonobuoys, with a flame float at the centre. As the first sonobuoy came on the air, it confirmed that there was indeed a U-boat in the area. With no further radar contact on the boat, the crew of the Liberator carried out a timed run from the flame float and released a couple of passive homing torpedoes at the point where the U-boat was thought to be. Six minutes later the sonobuoy operator heard a long reverberating sound in his earphones, and after that there were only sea noises. It was slim evidence of a kill, but when German records were checked after the war it became clear that U-905 had gone missing in approximately that position at that time.

Those two incidents, I think, can be thought of as establishing the boundaries of the huge advance in operational technique made by Coastal Command during the Second World War.

THE INTRODUCTION OF RADAR

In 1939 the Coastal Command crews had only their eyes to detect enemy U-boats or friendly shipping. Oversea navigation was a hit-and-miss business and all too often aircraft failed to find the convoys they were supposed to escort. During the first couple of years of the war the U-boat crews regarded the British air patrols as an irritant that imposed few constraints on their operations. Clearly the Command had a long way to go if it was to impose any serious threat against its elusive prey.

The first important technical development to alter that picture was the metric wavelength radar, the ASV Mark I which entered service early in 1940. The equipment operated on frequencies in the 200 MHz band. Initially it gave disappointing results, for serviceability was poor. And even when the device was serviceable, often it was not used properly. Initially the operation of the radar was shared between the navigator and the wireless operator, and this task was secondary to their normal duties. The radar operator's position was situated wherever there happened to be room to spare in the aircraft – in some types the radar operator had to sit on the lid of the Elsan chemical toilet, which he had to leave if anyone wanted it for its original purpose. Under operational conditions the early radars could detect a surfaced U-boat at a maximum of only about $3\frac{1}{2}$ miles. Indeed at first the main – and significant – value of radar was for locating convoys in poor visibility – they could be detected at ranges of up to 12 miles. The device was also useful for assisting navigation – coastlines could be seen at ranges of 20 miles or more.

During 1941 the somewhat improved ASV Mark II radar entered service. This was also a metric wavelength equipment, but with an additional sideways-looking antenna array it could detect surfaced U-boats on the surface at ranges of up to 12 miles.

NEW WEAPONS

As we have seen, at the beginning of the war the RAF's anti-submarine bombs were as dangerous to the aircraft dropping them as they were to the enemy U-boats. The weapons were fundamentally unsuitable for their intended task. The only readily-available alternative was the 450 pound naval depth charge, which was modified for air use by the fitting of a streamlined nose cap and an air tail. This thin-cased weapon had a higher charge-to-weight ratio than the anti-submarine bomb, giving a greater blast effect. And, more important, the hydrostatic fuse would detonate the weapon only when it reached a set depth below the surface, thus removing a major hazard to the aircraft that dropped it. The new depth charge entered service in Coastal Command in the summer of 1940.

OPERATIONAL RESEARCH SECTION (ORS)

In March 1941 Professor Patrick Blackett became Scientific Advisor to the AOC-in-C, and formed the Coastal Command Operational Research Section. Professor E. Williams, whose previous post had been working on theoretical studies at Farnbrough on a magnetic proximity fuse for depth charges, became his assistant. One of their first tasks was to analyse the attacks made by aircraft on U-boats to date. Although the depth charge was a clear improvement over the AS bomb, the results were still unsatisfactory: only about one per cent of the air attacks resulted in the U-boat being assessed as 'definitely sunk', and a further $2\frac{1}{2}$ per cent as 'probably sunk'.

The depth charges were set to exploded at a depth of between 100 and 150 feet, which was the average the boat was expected to reach if it started its dive at the average distance at which an aircraft would be seen. Williams found that in as many as 40 per cent of attacks the U-boat was either on the surface or had been out of sight for less than a quarter of a minute. In other words, the depth charges were set to explode far too deep. Williams saw that what was needed was not a magnetic proximity fuse – which would have taken many months to develop – but a shallower setting for the depth charges. He calculated that the optimum depth of detonation should be 20 feet; that setting was not possible on the modified Naval depth charges, whose minimum setting was 50 feet. And work began at top priority to develop a genuine shallow setting depth charge. That was the first of several coups by ORS during the war.

IMPROVED AIRCRAFT

During the first two years of the war there had been a major improvement in the patrol aircraft operated by Coastal Command. The Ansons were replaced by the more effective and longer ranging Hudsons, Whitleys and Wellingtons. There were far more Sunderland flying boats, and the American Catalina long-range flying boat was also available in small numbers. Finally, and most important of all, the first squadron was in the process of re-equipping with modified version of the B-24 Liberator bomber with additional fuel tanks to enable it to spend two hours on task at a distance of more than a thousand miles from base. About threequarters of the aircraft assigned to anti-submarine patrol units now had radar, and all were armed with depth charges.

Not until the summer of 1942 did a genuine shallow setting firing pistol become available and this was fitted to the new 250 pound depth charge. The change was immediately obvious to the U-boat crews, and those who survived attacks reported that the enemy was using weapons with a larger explosive charge or a much more powerful explosive, or perhaps both.

NIGHT ATTACK ON SUBMARINES

Thus far, U-boats recharging their batteries on the surface at night were relatively safe from air attack. Aircraft could detect them on radar, but the target was usually lost in the mass of sea clutter well before it came within sight of the pilot. As an answer to the night attack problem, Squadron Leader Humphrey Leigh designed the so-called 'Leigh Light'. In its initial production form this was a 24-inch Naval carbon searchlight modified to fit in the retractable belly gun turret of the Wellington bomber. The aircraft carried out the initial part of its attack run using radar, and the searchlight operator turned on the light just before the target disappeared into the sea clutter on the radar screen. During the final part of the attack run the operator held the narrow beam on the target by means of a hydraulic control system.

The first night attack on a submarine using a Leigh Light took place in June 1942, and the following month the first 'kill' was achieved using the device. In the weeks that followed several U-boats running through the Bay of Biscay on the surface at night suffered damage or were sunk.

The German answer to the new threat was to fit U-boats with the so called Metox equipment, what we would now call a radar warning receiver, to provide warning of the approach aircraft making radar homings. By mid-September a large proportion of the U-boats carried the new receiver, and thereafter the number of night attacks on these craft fell sharply.

CENTIMETRIC WAVELENGTH RADAR

The next major development in the conflict was the introduction of the British ASV Mark III and the American SCR 517 radars, both of which were centimetric wavelength equipments working in what we would now call the DE band. As well as giving 360 degree cover, these radars had the great advantage of operating on frequencies that were far outside the coverage of the U-boats' Metox receivers. During February 1943 aircraft carrying the new radars took part in patrols over the Bay of Biscay, and in the months that followed the U-boat command received a disturbing stream of reports from U-boat crews who had suffered air attacks while on the surface at night, with no warning from the Metox receivers.

At top priority the German Navy tried to develop an effective centimetric wavelength warning receiver for its U-boats. But German research in high frequency technology lagged far behind that of the western Allies and the first German centimetric wavelength radar warning receiver, code-named the Naxos-U, did not enter service until October 1943. It proved highly unreliable. In order to get it into service rapidly, there was no attempt to route the aerial cable through the pressure hull. When the boat surfaced one of the crew carried the aerial topsides and clipped it on to the conning tower. A length of co-axial cable led from the aerial, through the conning tower hatch, to the receiver in the U-boat's radio room. It required only one careless sailor to plant his size 9 boot on the cable, and the latter's ability to convey the radar signals was much impaired. The makeshift system was not good enough, and not until the spring of 1944 was a properly engineered centimetric warning receiver available for U-boats.

The German Navy saw that the real answer to the threat of attack from aircraft carrying centimetric-wavelength radar was the installation of Schnorkel equipment to all operational U-boats. In the summer of 1943 it initiated a crash programme to fit the device, but this took much longer than originally planned. By the time of D-Day, 6 June 1944, only six boats fitted with this equipment were available for the attack on ships taking part in the Allied seaborne invasion. The Schnorkel was difficult to detect on radar and it gave the U-boat a high degree of immunity to air attack. But the device did little to protect them from the overwhelming Allied surface patrols and they were able to achieve little.

COUNTERING THE SUBMERGED SUBMARINE

Following the entry of the USA into the war in December 1941, the US and British scientific efforts to develop new systems to counter the U-boat were dovetailed. In general, the British scientists and engineers concentrated on improving systems already in service or working those that could enter service in the short term. The Americans, with their greater reserve of uncommitted scientific capacity, concentrated on the longer term projects.

From mid-1943 on three American-developed airborne systems entered service to assist in the attack of submerged U-boats: the passive homing torpedo, code-named the 'Mark 24 mine'; the Magnetic Anomaly Detector, or MAD equipment, and the radio Sonobuoy. During the next couple of years these devices would play a useful part in the anti-U-boat war, though the older systems would account for the majority of U-boats sunk from the air during the remainder of the conflict.

In this discussion I have concentrated on the development of hardware. But, as I sure everyone in this room will appreciate, the new systems would have been of little use without parallel and long running training effort to enable aircrews to get the most out of the equipment, and without the hard work and skill of the ground crews to keep it serviceable.

8. A German Perspective

Dr Jurgen Rohwer

When we look at the roles air forces had in the Battle of the Atlantic and especially in the U-boat War, there is no question that the most important part in this fight of aircraft with or against U-boats is connected with RAF Coastal Command. So the main part of my paper is concerned with its operations and the reactions of the German U-boat and Luftwaffe commands. We also have to include in this analysis the shore-based squadrons of the Dominion air forces, the squadrons manned by Allied personnel under RAF control and the shore based squadrons of the US Navy and the US Army Air Force.

Nor must we forget the carrier planes of the Royal Navy and the US escort carriers. We must mention too the effects of the attacks against U-boat connected targets by RAF Bomber Command and the 8th US Army Air Force, and last but not least the effects of the minelaying offensive of Bomber Command in the Bay of Biscay and the Baltic and their consequences for the Battle of the Atlantic.

Let us start by looking at the German use of aircraft to support the operations of the U-boats.

When the Führer der Unterseeboote, the then Captain Karl Dönitz, started from 1937 to 1939 with the development of his operational concept of group or 'wolf-pack' attacks against the escorted convoys he clearly saw the problem of finding them with the insufficient number of U-boats then available. So in the manoeuvres in the Baltic in 1938/39 aircraft were already being used for reconnaissance. But when the war started in 1939 there were no aircraft available in the Luftwaffe which could reach the operational areas to the west of the British Isles and the Bay of Biscay. So the first phase of the U-boat war up to the conquest of

Norway and France in June 1940 was fought without any co-operation between the Luftwaffe and the U-boats.

Then, although the Norwegian and French bases were operational from July 1940 onwards, it took several months more before the I Group/Kampf-Geschwader 40 got its 12 long-range Focke-Wulf 200 Condor planes and was by order of Hitler in early January 1941 put under operational control of the Commander U-boats. The planes had to fly from Bordeaux west of Ireland to Stavanger and back on the next day. Seldom were more than one or two planes operational each day and their reconnaissance signals were difficult to use because of bad position fixing. This was improved only when the Condors sent homing signals which were evaluated by D/F from shore stations and U-boats to give the other U-boats the position of the convoy. So in spring 1941 the U-boats more usually homed in Condor-flights in order to attack the convoys. From 8 to 12 February 1941 U 37 led five Condors and the cruiser ADMIRAL HIPPER to convoys HG.53 and SLS.64, and together they sank 16 of their 25 ships. Again on the night of 26 February U-47 sank three vessels of convoy OB.290 and damaged one tanker before homing in six Condors which sank seven more ships and damaged four others.

But when in March the Sunderlands of Coastal Command forced the U-boats to operate more to the west, the area was outside the range of the Condors and the co-operation was only re-opened in July/August when the U-boats started to attack the Gibraltar convoys, often supported successfully by the reconnaissance reports of the Condors which in turn became endangered by the planes of the first escort carrier AUDACITY, a captured and rebuilt former German freighter.

In the fourth phase in the first part of 1942 the U-boats operated off the American coast far outside the range of German aircraft, and this did not change when the Commander U-boats shifted the main operational area again to the North Atlantic convoy route. In autumn 1942 the increased use of Allied four-engined aircraft against the transit route of the U-boats in the Bay of Biscay led to the transfer of some Ju-88 CVI long-range fighters but they could not achieve air superiority against the counter-deployment of British Beaufighters and Mosquitos with disastrous consequences during the Battle of the Bay in summer 1943.

The use of He 177 and Do-217 planes with guided bombs Hs-293 from August 1943 forced the British convoys and the U-boat hunting 'support groups' to the west, facilitating the U-boats passage of the Biscay. But when the few newly available Very Long Range BV 222 and Ju 290 aircraft tried to help the U-boats find the convoys in October 1943/February 1944 they failed because the old U-boats were no longer able to gain attacking positions against the omnipresent air cover.

Only the new fast Type XXI electro-boats might have been able to gain such positions submerged, supported by the very fast recce-version of the Do-335, but neither system was operational up to the end of the war.

I will now concentrate on the use of shore-based planes against the U-boats with some brief asides on the role of carrier-based planes.

Because of the official assumption that the U-boat menace might be controlled by the use of ASDIC the anti-submarine (A/S) role of Coastal Command had no priority. Moreover, as the last of the combat commands behind Bomber and Fighter Commands, it was equipped mostly with obsolete planes, and there was no great investment in the development of new and efficient A/S weapons. There were only two squadrons of the modern Sunderland flying boats suitable for long-range patrols against U-boats, and most of the other planes were old flying boats; about 200 of the 265 total were only of short range.

No wonder that under such conditions the German U-Boats experienced, apart from some surprise attacks, no great danger from the shore-based aircraft during the first two phases of the Battle of the Atlantic up to early 1941. When the real 'wolf pack' operations started against the convoys in autumn 1940 aircraft had neither the range nor the means to interfere with surfaced U-boats in their night attacks off the North Channel. From March 1940 to March 1941 Coastal Command flew 51,333 hours of convoy escort and support and 59,830 hours of A/S and recce patrols. 108 U-boats were sighted and 86 attacked, but only two U-boats were sunk by ships with assistance from aircraft.

It took up to the spring of 1941 before Coastal Command received more modern planes of sufficient range. To add to the Sunderlands came the Wellingtons, the American Catalina flying boats and finally the first nine Liberators for 120 Squadron which could be modified to the Very Long Range mode. In addition more effective depth charges became available and more and more planes were equipped with ASVII radar. The intensified air coverage of the area off the North Channel forced the U-boats out to the west in their operations. While the direct effects of attacks from the air were still limited, the indirect effect of forcing the U-boats out into the spacious areas of the Central North Atlantic had a great influence on the first and – in my opinion – decisive crisis in the U-boat War.

Up to the summer of 1941 the U-boats in the operational areas – rarely more than 10-15 at a time – had great problems in finding the convoys. Then when the British broke into the radio traffic between the Commander U-boats and his U-boats at sea first by using captured cipher materials and from August onwards by decrypting the signals in cipher 'Heimisch' with cryptanalytical methods, even the slowly rising number of U-boats was insufficient to overcome the effective routeing of convoys around the German patrol lines by the Admiralty's Submarine Tracking Room.

The U-boats now found convoys only when an approaching or returning U-boat by chance met one and could call other boats in to the attack, something that ULTRA never could prevent. By cautious calculation I found that during these six months between 1.5 to 2 million gross tons of Allied shipping were saved by the re-routeing of convoys, one of the most decisive factors in the whole Battle of the Atlantic!

In the fourth phase in January 1942 operation 'Paukenschlag' shifted the focal area of the U-boat war to the US East Coast. There the U-boats encountered an unexpectedly weak defence. Notwithstanding the experiences of the US Atlantic Fleet during its three months of active participation in the North Atlantic convoy operations as far away as the area south of Iceland, it took more than five months before the US Navy introduced convoys off the East Coast. This led to terrible losses of independently sailing merchant ships.

During this time the German U-boats had almost nothing to fear from shorebased aircraft, because no experienced US Navy squadrons of A/S planes were made available and the civilian pilots with their unsuitable planes were incapable of doing anything worthwhile. The reports of the U-boats led Admiral Dönitz to his remark: "The aeroplane can no more eliminate the U-boat than a crow can fight a mole."'

But when the number of targets dropped off sharply after the introduction of coastal convoys and he had to transfer the main effort of his U-boats in the fifth phase back to the North Atlantic convoy route in July 1942, he had soon to change his mind. While the wolf pack operations against the convoys had up to the end of the year not too much to fear from the air because they were fought in the 'air gap' between the ranges of Allied aircraft from Newfoundland, Iceland and Northern Ireland, the danger now arose in the transit area of the Bay of Biscay which the U-boats had to pass on their way from and to the bases in Western France.

It was the custom of the German U-boats to traverse the Bay submerged by day and to re-charge the batteries only at night when the aircraft of 19 Group in Southwest England could not see them running surfaced. This had worked well, but in June and July reports started to come in of surprise attacks by night, sometimes with a searchlight illuminating the U-boat. Up to this time the German experts, who had now acknowledged the existence of Funkmess on Allied surface vessels, still doubted that the British could equip their aircraft with radar antennas as they could find no clear evidence of this in the reports of the U-boats. But now they had to accept that the reason for such night attacks could only be radar location.

In fact Coastal Command had been using its ASV-MkII radar since October 1940, but the detection range against a surfaced U-boat was only eight to ten miles, so that by day in normal weather conditions a U-boat observed a plane early enough to dive in time; moreover in a sea above strength four and below a distance of about four miles the echoes of the sea-clutter covered the U-boat so that no precise night attack was possible. This problem was overcome in June 1942 by the introduction of the Leigh Light into five Wellingtons of 172 Squadron. Their surprise attacks caused a growing radar scare on the German side by giving the experts and the U-boat Command a plausible explanation not only for the attacks but also for the many difficulties the U-boats had experienced in intercepting convoys. They thought – wrongly as we know now – that the patrol lines were located by radar-equipped planes. This radar-scare blacked out the probably then more important ship-borne HF/DF which enabled an escort to home on a contact signal and force the U-boat to dive so that it lost contact. And even more important, the radar scare silenced many questions about the security of the communications. This indirect effect of the new Allied equipment was more influential in the long run than the real losses and damage caused by the air attacks.

The German U-boat Command ordered some countermeasures. The U-boats now had to pass through the Bay at night submerged and to surface for recharging the batteries at daylight when the aircraft could be observed in time by optical means. In addition the first improvised search receiver Metox was introduced in September, reducing the aircraft sightings almost immediately by about 60%. But the 30 JU 88CVI long-range fighters sent to KG.40 gave only short relief and were no match for the Beaufighters introduced by Coastal Command over the Bay as a countermeasure.

But not only was German attention concentrated on the situation in the Bay transit area; Coastal Command too concentrated its efforts there against the traversing U-boats, where ULTRA was still giving good information from decryption of the cipher 'Hydra' used by the patrol vessels escorting the U-boats in and out. The 'black out' with the 'Triton'-cipher deprived the Allies of exact information about the U-boat patrol lines in the mid-Atlantic air gap, making it difficult to direct the very few available VLR-planes to the right spot in time.

The U-boats – now refuelled between their operations in remote sea areas by U-tankers – from July to December 1942 attacked many convoys in this air gap. But notwithstanding the experience that even heavily attacked convoys – like SC 107 in November and HX 217 in December – were saved from further losses by the arrival of only one or two planes, the Allied commands with incomprehensible negligence refrained from strengthening the only five operational VLR Liberators of 120 Squadron in Iceland and other squadrons in Northern Ireland and Newfoundland with more such aircraft. Instead the 32 Liberators transferred to Coastal Command between July and September were not modified to VLR-standard but sent to 224 and 59 Squadrons in Southwest England to strengthen the Bay patrols, as were the additional 19 planes and the two A/S squadrons of the US Army Air Force that came under Coastal Command's control from November 1942 to January 1943.

The airmen followed their preconception that their offensive tactics of 'search, find and kill' were more destructive to the U-boats than the defensive cover flights above the convoys. And when in March 1943 operational research analyses, ordered by the new C-in-C of Coastal Command, Air Marshal Slessor, gave evidence that the flight time for sighting a U-boat near a convoy was only about one tenth of the time spent in A/S patrols against the transit routes, inter-service rivalries and in-fights between the air and sea commanders in the Atlantic and Pacific prevented fast allocation of VLR Liberators from the great stocks in the USA. Only in March to May 1943 did 120 and 86 Squadrons in Northern

Ireland and Iceland and 10 Squadron RCAF in Newfoundland each receive their 15 VLR-Liberators.

Similar problems arose with the allocation of the 20 US and British escort carriers commissioned up to the end of 1942. It took up to March 1943 before the first of them was used on the North Atlantic route to help close the air gap, and two more came only in May when the battle was almost over.

In the first eleven weeks of 1943 the U-boat offensive reached its highest mark. With the new break into the German cipher TRITON the Submarine Tracking rooms started again to route the convoys around the German patrol lines. But when in February and March the number of German U-boats on the convoy routes rose to 40, 50 and 60 there were sometimes up to four patrol lines and convoy routeing became more and more impractical. This was the more so as – unknown to the British at the time – the German cryptanalytic service, the xB-Dienst, was able to decrypt many signals in Naval Cipher No. 3, used to direct the convoys and their escorts and to send the daily U-boat situation reports to the convoys. So Allied re-routeing orders could often be countered by re-direction of patrol lines. The biggest convoy battles of the war in March were the consequence when four east-going convoys lost 20% of their ships during a short black-out in ULTRA caused by the introduction of a new weather code book depriving Bletchley Park of the source for cribs. To overcome the crisis, which threatened to break down the whole convoy system, the backbone of the Allied strategy to win the U-boat war, Bletchley Park concentrated all its efforts. When this was successfully achieved after only about twelve days, a new operational use of the ULTRA information was started.

It was a great surprise to the German U-boat Command that after its biggest success in a Geleitzugschlacht no more operations of this kind were possible and this with the number of U-boats greater than ever and with the xB-Dienst most successful in decrypting the Allied routeing signals, thus enabling the Commander U-boats to shift his patrol lines quickly across the ordered route. Notwithstanding the fact that almost 60% of the convoys on the North Atlantic route were contacted by U-boats, the 'wolf packs' were prevented by the sea and air escorts from gathering for mass attacks and driven off or forced to dive. And the losses rose to an intolerable level so that Commander U-boats was forced on 24 May to break off convoy operations in the North Atlantic.

In his contemporary analysis he ascribed almost 75% of the 31 U-boat losses of the last four weeks to air attacks, but he saw only 38% of these losses occurring in actual convoy battles. And he saw the reason for the steep rise in losses as "the superiority of the enemy radar equipment, which enables him to surprise our boats from the air while they are waiting in the operational area or are homeward or outward bound".

This greatly overestimated the role of radar in this phase of the campaign and was mistaken in evaluating the relation between the direct and indirect results of air operations. For instance, during the big operation against convoys HX 229 and SC 122 in March, of 29 U-boats reported by aircraft only one was found by radar and 28 were sighted by optical means. At this time the fear that the aircraft might be equipped with location devices not detectable by the Metox search receiver was clearly exaggerated, because the equipping of planes with the new 9.1 cm radar ASV-III had only started in February 1943 and did not come into general use until later in the year.

While only 14 U-boats of the 31 were really sunk by aircraft instead of the assumed 23, and only 7 by air when in contact with a convoy, the real problem with the air escort of convoys was that ULTRA enabled the Allied commmands to operate the relatively few VLR Liberators of 10 Squadron RCAF from Newfoundland and 120 and 86 Squadrons of 15 Group from Iceland and Northern Ireland; at the same time it enabled the first three escort carriers to escort and support only those convoys in real danger from wolf packs and to close for them the air gap. In the same way the first five surface 'support groups' were used to fight the endangered convoys through or round the wolf packs. So it became impossible for the U-boats to race around a convoy on the surface in order to gain a favourable attack position. They were repeatedly forced to dive and therefore sagged far astern.

To the Commander U-boats the only way open was to switch the main area of operations to outside the air cover and to try to equip the U-boats with weapons to counter the radar, the aircraft and the surface escorts. These comprised a search receiver which was also effective against frequencies not so far covered; strong anti-aircraft armament; and the homing torpedo, which would enable convoy operations to be renewed in the North Atlantic up to the time when the true fast submarines now on order became ready.

But from ULTRA the Allies recognised immediately that the North Atlantic had been evacuated and shifted the main strength of

Coastal Command's A/S squadrons to 19 Group in South-west England for a massive air offensive against the U-boat transit routes in the Bay of Biscay. When the Commander U-boats tried to counter this by ordering the U-boats to proceed through the Bay in groups of three to five so as to support each other with their anti-aircraft armament this only led to the A/S aircraft being concentrated against the groups. They now used their ASV-III radar, combined in many squadrons with the Leigh Light and the acoustic homing torpedo, cover-named 'Mark XXIV mine'.

At the same time the operations in more distant areas where the defences were weaker had only short-lived successes, because the Americans used their hunter-killer groups with escort carriers to hunt down the supply U-boats at their replenishment points, which were known from decrypted radio signals of the Commander U-boats; they were also using the American version of the Mark XXIV mine and the 'Fido' torpedo. Again ULTRA enabled the Allies to use their still not too strong forces in the most effective way, giving the Germans the impression of overwhelming strength.

The Commander U-boats was determined to renew the convoy operations on the North Atlantic route using the available Type VII U-boats with the 'Wanz' or 'Naxos' search receiver, strong AA armament and the acoustic homing torpedo Zaunkönig. With great relief he saw in August the first new group, Leuthen, pass submerged through the Bay with almost no interference from the air during the surfaced recharging. This seemed to underline the fear that Metox radiations might have been the source of the Allied surprise air attacks, a mistake reinforced by the statement of an air POW. The first operation of the Leuthen group seemed to represent an outstanding success for the new Zaunkönig torpedo and the new tactic of fighting back against the air escort, an error which had grave consequences during the following weeks when operations were completely unsuccessful and accompanied by heavy losses inflicted by the convoys' sea and air escorts. Again ULTRA was of great help to the Allies, first in enabling the air squadrons to be switched back to the convoy routes, and then in concentrating the VLR planes and the support groups with the escort carriers around those convoys that were in danger from wolf packs. The Commander U-boats was forced to give up his attempts at radio-controlled group operations against convoys; these faded out in the first weeks of 1944.

The Commander U-boats nevertheless decided to continue with the U-boat operations for the following reasons. He hoped to renew the anti-convoy operations later in 1944 using the new Type XXI U-boats with their high submerged speed, their active and passive radar equipment, their new AA armament and especially their new guided torpedoes with a fast reloading system and new fire control computers. In the meantime the old U-boats had to continue in a reduced way to tie down the Allied A/S forces which might otherwise be used for attacks against German coastal traffic and – in the case of the long-range aircraft – for strengthening the bomber offensive against German cities. He also thought such operations necessary to keep up-to-date the experience against Allied A/S weapons and methods.

The intention to gain experience with the new Schnorkel breathing tube, which would enable the old U-boats to remain submerged even when re-charging their batteries, was frustrated by the loss of the first few U-boats that were so equipped; by the delays in bringing the Schnorkel equipment from the factories to the French repair yards owing to the damage to the railway system caused by the Allied air interdiction campaign in preparation of the big landing in France; and by the necessity to hold the Schnorkel-equipped boats at stand-by in their French or Norwegian bases for operations against the awaited landings.

When operation OVERLORD started there was so big a concentration of A/S air squadrons west of the Channel entrance, flying in groups by day and with radar and Leigh Light by night, that it was absolutely impossible for U-boats without Schnorkel to proceed into the Channel. All those which did try were heavily attacked by aircraft and sunk or damaged so that they had to return or were recalled by the Commander U-boats. Only the Schnorkel U-boats could evade the air attacks but they had to face the several strong surface A/S groups concentrated in the Channel entrance and only very few were able after a fortnight to enter the 'funnel' where they only achieved minimal successes.

With the breakout of the Allied armies from the bridgehead in Normandy the Germans were forced to evacuate the bases in Western France. The transfer of the operational U-boats from France to Norway was accomplished with surprisingly low losses, because the U-boats could go submerged and the aircraft were unable to locate the Schnorkel-heads in the sea-clutter when they were used at night for re-charging the batteries.

The Schnorkel-U-boats which the Commander U-boats sent into the Channel and into the coastal waters of Great Britain from August 1944 onwards reported to be able to stay in these areas for weeks without being detected by aircraft or surface A/S groups. Even when they attacked single ships or convoys and escort vessels tried to hunt them to death, they could often evade pursuit by using the density layers in coastal waters which reflected the sonar beams. And now HF/DF was only of limited use, because the U-boats received their orders before departure or by radio signals in special cipher settings for individual boats which like one-time-pads could not be broken by analytical means.

The U-boats were, however, almost stationary and could not move to intercept the traffic. They had mainly to wait for the targets to come their way, because the air coverage was so dense and the surface A/S groups were so efficient. Finally in early 1945 the air and surface A/S forces swamped the areas around the British Isles, inflicting such heavy losses on the U-boats that they were forced out of the coastal waters.

The new Type XXI U-boats, which were causing great fear on the British side up to early 1945, could not be made operational before the end of the war, so their efficiency against the then available A/S forces was never tested. The reason for this had much to do with the operations of RAF Bomber Command, whose influence on the U-boat war now requires some comment.

For Bomber Command the campaign against the U-boats was always a secondary task, distracting its aircraft from the strategic air offensive against Germany. The Admiralty's requests for attacks on the U-boat bases were almost always looked at with great reservations, and a great opportunity was missed to attack the German U-boat bunkers in France while they were being built. It was after the Casablanca Conference which put the victory over the U-boats at the top of the priority list that attacks against the French bases were finally undertaken by RAF Bomber Command and the 8th US Army Air Force in the first five months of 1943, but these only led to heavy losses in aircraft, great destruction of the French cities and severe casualties among the civilian population, but not one U-boat was sunk or damaged, because they were now protected by the finished bunkers. The attacks were then called off.

Even the heavy attacks against the German port cities of Hamburg, Bremen and Kiel in 1943 and 1944 achieved no real destruction of the building yards and damaged only relatively few U-boats on the slipways or in the fitting out basins.

The main delays in U-boat construction were caused by the absence of yard-workers after heavy raids when they tried to find new lodgings for their families. Some raids which hit factories supplying the building yards in other cities also caused delays.

Only in late 1944 and 1945 did the strategic air attacks cause major delays in the building programmes for the new types of U-boat, mainly by damaging the transportation that supplied the assembly yards with the prefabricated sections, but also by destroying new boats or damaging them beyond repair.

Bomber Command's minelaying offensive against the Biscay ports was a limited success as far as the transit of U-boats was concerned, and the German mine-sweeping forces escorted more than 3600 U-boats with only three losses up to 1944. Of course the mine-sweeping effort was a heavy task and consumed a great deal of resources. More influential was the minelaying offensive against the Baltic in 1944 and 1945, not so much because of the losses inflicted but more so by the delays in the training programmes caused by the need to block the training areas or the swept traffic channels while the mine-sweeping forces were trying to sweep the mines.

If we ask in conclusion what were the most important contributions of shore-based aircraft to the victory over the U-boats I want to mention three points:

a. In spring 1941 RAF Coastal Command forced the U-boats away from the focal points off the North Channel into the open ocean, where first the few U-boats had difficulties in finding the convoys and where in the second half year of 1941 it was possible to route the convoys round the patrol lines with the use of ULTRA.

b. In the spring of 1943 ULTRA made it possible to close the air gap in the North Atlantic for those convoys in danger from U-boat patrol lines by the allocation of not more than 45 VLR Liberators and three escort carriers, so turning the tide only eight weeks after the catastrophic convoy battles of March.

c. In late 1944 and early 1945 the massive attacks of Bomber Command and the 8th US Army Air Force on the U-boat yards and the transport system, together with Bomber Command's mining offensive in the Baltic, prevented the new types of U-boat becoming operational before the end of the war.

But there remain certain big questions for us historians:

a. Why were the Allied leaders unable to allocate the crucial VLR planes and escort carriers to the North Atlantic area earlier and in sufficient numbers from the available stocks?

b. Why did Bomber Command neglect for so long the possibility of destroying the U boat pens while they were under construction?

c. Why did Bomber Command not devastate earlier the U-boat yards instead of the cities?

9. Pre-lunch discussion

The pre-lunch session was opened to comments and questions, Sir Edward Chilton commenced the discussion:-

It would be unusual for something like this to conclude without my having something to say. Earl Mountbatten once paid me the great compliment of calling me the 'Bomber Harris' of Coastal Command. I hope naval officers present will not be offended by anything I say – I have always been regarded as a great friend of the Admiralty but there were times when my friendship was stretched to the limit.

There has been some talk of World War I – there were lots of excellent lessons from here but they were ignored by the Air Force and the Admiralty especially lessons about the submarines being able to approach and attack at night, but I would make one very important observation. When the RAF was formed every naval aviator except one left the Navy and joined the RAF. Cochrane was one of them; he became one of our finest chiefs – I wish he had been in Coastal.

Let us turn to the beginning of the war. You would hardly credit it, but people in Whitehall did not know what was required to feed the people in Britain; it was not until after the war, when a committee was set up – I was the senior RAF member; Wilf Oulton my No. 2 – and we were asked to do an assessment for the future. We said we must first find out what this country needed by way of food, fuel and other things. If the Germans had adopted different bombing and mining tactics from the start, if they had bombed and mined our ports such as London – to which so much had come before the war – and Liverpool, we could not have unloaded our ships. As it was, our ships had an appalling turn-round period and our repair yards were hopeless – everyone downed tools at the slightest bombing. But for the introduction of the Liberty ships from America we would have been up the gum tree – eventually one ship was being built every six weeks. When Admiral Raeder heard of this he felt they would lose the war, for our ability to replace our ships was faster than their ability to sink them.

Another thing you would hardly credit was that in mid 1941 the Admiralty said "we must take over Coastal Command lock stock and barrel"; you can imagine the confusion this caused. Sound judgement eventually prevailed and after a few weeks it cooled down, for the War Office said "if you're going to have your Air Force we must have ours". They put in an enormous shopping list for what they proposed as an Army Air Force. Ultimately the Admiralty were given operational control of Coastal Command and it worked out well.

Captain Peyton-Ward has been mentioned; he was a very gifted ex-submariner, much loathed by the Admiralty curiously enough, which is why we got him as their liaison officer. He turned out to be first-class for Coastal Command; he understood the German mind, he understood submarines – and we couldn't have got on without him.

Lord Shackleton and I are the last of the people who were on the ULTRA list; what we should have done without ULTRA I do not know.

The Admiralty themselves were not fully behind the convoy concept all the time. When it got a bit better, sometime in '41, they became less enthusiastic about all the ships that we required to defend convoys; Churchill too became a bit unenthusiastic and said maybe we were putting too many resources into this. Later, of course, it got much worse. The Trade Division of the Admiralty had an uphill fight to get the convoy battle solved, and to stop the 'independent' ships – all ships over 20 knots – going their own way. We had terrible losses among these.

Professor Rohwer referred to Bomber Command's failure to bomb the pens. But it was Churchill really – he was siding all the time with Harris, wanting him to bomb Germany, so he was lukewarm about the bombing of the pens. Harris of course didn't become C-in-C Bomber Command until early 1942 and was given the brief to build up the force to attack Germany. He should, however, have released the Lancasters that had the radial engines – the Mark II. They were not really popular in Bomber Command and properly handled, modified to take more fuel, they could have done almost as well as the Liberator. A few squadrons of those would have made all the difference earlier on.

On Schnorkels, I was at 19 Group concerned with U-boat Channel operations. The Schnorkel operation had a tough time. One submarine gave up the unequal struggle, went into Lyme Bay and gave up, because they had been diving and the operator had done the wrong thing, sucking the air out of the submarine instead.

A study of the German U-boat logs showed that at least half their commanders didn't see a convoy. Think what would have happened if all had seen and attacked one. I don't know the reason – it was either the weather or bad navigation.

During the Norwegian invasion period the German torpedoes were hopeless they hit all sorts of ships but didn't explode. The German Admiralty made a great fuss about this; they had a bad period too in 1943. Ours went off very well – HMS TRINIDAD torpedoed somebody and the torpedo went round in a circle and hit TRINIDAD.

In a subsequent note Sir Edward reminded the Society of the dire effects on home food rations of the merchant ship sinkings by U-boats, disruption of shipping to ports etc. He quoted a report by Lord Woolton of the War Cabinet in mid-December 1940 as follows:

UK stocks were only

Wheat	enough for 15 weeks
Meat	Two weeks only (Ration of one shilling a week per person)
Butter	Eight weeks (on ration)
Margarine	Three weeks (on ration)
Bacon	27 weeks (on ration)
Imported fruit	Finished

Group Captain Richardson. Dr Price referred to the Introduction of 450 lb depth charges. I commanded a squadron in 1941 and we carried sticks of six Torpex 250lb depth charges – I do not remember anyone carrying 450 pounders.

Dr Price. The initial depth charge for the RAF was 450lb but it was soon replaced by the 250lb.

Sqn Ldr Bulloch. I agree. We did have 450lb depth charges right at the beginning of 1941 and they were a dead loss; they used to go off on impact with the water.

Lord Shackleton. Dr Rohwer, you gave us a lot of information about the Mark 21 U-boat, but nothing about the Walther boat; the Walther boat was a matter of great concern to Coastal, and at one time the aircrew all saw mysterious swirls which suggested the Walther boat was at sea. We in ULTRA knew it wasn't because we knew the exact state of play. There was great hope on the German side that it would be an important factor. Another question – how far were the U-boat commanders instructed to fire at crews in lifeboats. Those of us who were involved admired them for their courage and their chivalry, but I believe there was an incident when Donitz ordered the U-boat commanders, in the interests of security, to machine-gun crews in lifeboats. There was only one such incident I believe – there was a report through ULTRA of a meeting at St Nazaire when U-boat commanders decided not to carry out this order.

Dr. Rohwer. The development of the Walter U-boat was started in 1938/39 and first tests were made with the experimental boat V80 from 1940-1942. In February 1942 a 600 ton Walter U-boat U 791 was ordered but then cancelled in order to build four smaller experimental boats of 277 or 236 tons (U 792-U 795) which were completed in November 1943 and April 1944 and started with tests. In January 1943 orders for 12 Type XVII Walter U-boats of 312 tons were placed with Germania, Kiel (U 1081-U 1092) and Blohm & Voss Hamburg (U 1405-U 1416), but only the first three Blohm-v-boats were completed in late 1944 and early 1945. The other boats were cancelled for the new fast Type XXI electro-boats as was the order for the first two big Walter U-boats of Type XVIII, U 796 and U 797. The rapid construction of Walter U-boats was impossible, so in September 1943 the main effort was placed on the Type XXI, a development of a fast electro-boat, based on Type XVIII. Finally in September 1944 100 real front-line Walter U-boats of 842 tons (Type XXVI) were ordered, but when the war ended only four of them had been started, but they were never completed.

Your other point probably relates to the consequences of the LACONIA incident, the so-called 'Laconia order'. This is a mistaken idea.

The German U-boats early in the war sometimes tried to rescue or supply boats with survivors. But when the orders for the armed Allied merchant ships to fire at the U-boats became known, this was discontinued. Sometimes the U-boats were asked to try to rescue captains or engineering officers of merchant ships and bring them as prisoners home for interrogation. The situation in the Atlantic with the danger from aircraft prevented many such efforts.

In September 1942 U 156 under Cd. Hartenstein sank the British troop transport LACONIA in the Central Atlantic. When Hartenstein realised that there were 1500 Italian prisoners on board, he sent a radio message in open English to ask any ships in the area to help rescue the survivors. He tried to put as many people on board his submarine and to tow the boats with Italian, British and Polish survivors to an ordered meeting point with other U-boats. A Liberator bomber of the USAAF in a transfer flight from Ascension to Africa sighted the U-boat and reported this to Ascension. The CO of the base there then ordered another Liberator to attack the U-boat. When Dönitz got the report of this attack he forbade by radio any rescue operations of ship's crews by U-boats. But he or the U-boat Command never ordered them to attack or machine-gun survivors at sea.

There was only one case when some survivors were hit, namely when U 852 under Lt. Cdr. Eck sank in the south Atlantic on 13 March 1944 a Greek freighter PELEUS and tried to destroy some debris from the sunken ship. Eck and the responsible members of his crew were after the war court-martialled at Hamburg by the British, sentenced to death and shot.

There were some other more serious cases in the Indian Ocean where three Japanese submarines, I-8, I-37 and I-26, sank the ships BRITISH CHIVALRY (22 February 1944), TJISALAK (26 March 1944), RICHARD HOVEY (29 March 1944) and JEAN NICOLET (2 July 1944), rescued survivors and afterwards killed them in an atrocious way. (This was a consequence of an order by the Commander of the South West Area Fleet, Vice Admiral Takasu).

These are the only known cases when U-boat crews killed survivors of sunken ships.

Flt. Lt. Bury. AVM Oulton mentioned the occupation of the Azores in 1943; what was its importance?

AVM Oulton. On the first night of operations there we sank one U-boat and that prevented a lot of U-boats going into the Gap.

10. Digest of the Group Discussions

After the formal presentations, those attending the seminar divided into discussion groups where the various issues raised could be considered in more detail and the recollections of those involved in the Battle could be given. Each group was chaired by a member of the College Directing Staff and included participants in the Battle of the Atlantic, naval and air historians, Bracknell staff and students and, in some cases, serving naval officers.

The proceedings were all recorded and subsequently transcribed. A small editorial team then compiled a Digest of what appeared to be the most significant contributions. Divided into five main sections, this Digest is reproduced below.

While every effort has been made to ensure that all statements included are accurately reported, the original transcription was not always easy. Thus, if the occasional error does appear, the editorial team can only apologise.

EDITORIAL TEAM
Mr. Edward Bishop
Mr. Sebastian Cox
Mr. Cecil James
Group Captain Ian Madelin
Captain John Moore RN
Air Commodore Henry Probert
Mr. Tony Richardson
Group Captain Andrew Thompson
Group Captain Geoffrey Thorburn

A) POLICIES, PRIORITIES AND POLITICS

Most groups devoted some time to the question of priorities, ie why, with so much emphasis on the bomber offensive and on preparations for an eventual campaign in NW Europe, resources for the air component of anti-submarine warfare were rarely given priority. *John Terraine* stressed that neither objective would be attainable if the Battle of the Atlantic were lost, and to an extent this was recognised by the formation of the Battle of the Atlantic Committee in March 1941. The Prime Minister usually took the chair of this unique Cabinet committee – the only one devoted to a particular campaign, and it was here that major policy questions – allocation of resources, target selection being examples – were argued and decided.

Air Marshal Steer observed that Coastal Command's role at the start of the war had reflected the way the priorities had been determined beforehand, with the building of the bomber and fighter forces. It was the classic case of not being able to back every horse in every race.

Corelli Barnett agreed, adding that there was also competition between rival incompetencies in terms of strategic choice. Coastal Command was a cinderella, and the Navy had also neglected ASW. On the other side the U-boat arm too had been a cinderella. Both sides had made crashing mistakes; who would win the race to repair them?

Dr Willmott felt that the low priority given to the Battle in 1940-42 was one of the black spots of wartime strategy but he observed that it had been essential to revitalise the army after Dunkirk to withstand the possible shock of invasion. The various options open to us in late 1940 merited scrutiny. Apart from the developments already set in train by the Navy – the building of escort vessels and the extension of the convoy system by mid-ocean refuelling – there were few alternatives. Air power offered the only means of taking offensive action against the German war machine and what would have been the effect, he asked, of the RAF disappearing from the skies of Europe so as to operate over the Atlantic. Such a diversion would certainly not have satisfied Churchill's offensive spirit. *Group Captain Madelin* quoted *Denis Richards* to the effect that it was not only Bomber Command that did not wish to lend resources to Coastal, but that the Navy too were not enthusiastic. They were still obsessed by the threat posed by the major German surface units and took the view that if extra air resources were going to be allocated to the maritime war then they should be directed against the surface threat rather than the U-boats. *Jock Gardner* supported that. They were not so much concerned with threats like the Bismarck at sea as by the Scharnhorst and Gneisenau in the French ports; it was only after they had scuttled back to Germany that they came off the target list.

Professor Rohwer also found the imbalance of resources between Coastal and Bomber Commands difficult to understand, given the life or death struggle being waged over the Atlantic lines of communications – especially as Churchill was well seized of its importance. He could only put it down to arguments over the higher direction of the war which put the emphasis on a strategic air campaign against German cities. He found it ironic that the allocation of only 45 VLR aircraft transformed the Atlantic air gap situation, though these represented only a very small proportion of the available bomber strength.

Squadron Leader Bulloch echoed this point in describing the feelings of his squadron when six B 17s, on which he and others had trained and ferried from America, were handed over to Bomber Command at a time – early 1941 – when they would have been immensely valuable in providing increased range over the eastern Atlantic. The B 17 he had ferried was shot down on its first mission – against maritime targets in Brest.

Dr Eric Grove put the question another way, asking what difference 100 Lancasters would have made to the bombing of Germany. He was not opposed to the strategic bombing offensive, but such a limited number of aircraft that were key assets to winning what everyone said after the event was the most important battle of the war should not have been held back. It was not just the RAF that was at fault – the USN wanted Liberators for the Pacific for example – but it did strike him as strange that we were sending hundreds of aircraft over Germany that could have made extremely good maritime patrol aircraft and could have closed the mid-Atlantic gap.

Air Commodore Probert observed that the discussion related to 1942, when the Americans had just come into the war and the Allied leadership had to decide whether it would be Germany first or Japan first; the key decision was made that the primary effort must be against Germany, and the only means by which the Americans could make a contribution reasonably rapidly to the German war was by bringing their air forces – so the 8th Air Force started to arrive. The one way in which we could have made it absolutely certain that the Americans would not do this in early 1942 would have been if we had started to backtrack on the build-up of Bomber Command, for which the modern aircraft were so essential. The older aircraft were obsolescent and had enormous shortcomings; of the new aircraft the Stirling was not all it was cracked up to be, so we needed the Halifax and above all the Lancaster – still relatively unproven. If we decided to continue along the road of building up the bomber force, a road that had been followed for a very long time, there was no way of turning round and depriving it of a substantial percentage of the very aircraft that it needed in the effort to become effective. That was why the decision was made that all the Lancasters were to go to Bomber Command. Having committed ourselves to that strategy – and despite plenty of pressure from the Navy and Coastal Command for these aircraft to be diverted to the Battle of the Atlantic – someone had to make the decision, "Where did the priority rest?" We could look back and say that maybe they got it wrong, but *Probert* was convinced that that was the fundamental reason that decided the British leadership – not just that of the Air Force. Incidentally no one could understand the politics of 1942 without recalling the vast extension of the war to the Far East, which we had denuded of resources. Although it had to have lower priority than Europe we could not leave it without anything. We just did not have enough.

Probert went on to ask whether the decision making in early 1942 about Bomber Command might have been related to the fact that the worst period in the Battle of the Atlantic appeared to be behind us. *Dr Grove* replied that up to the end of 1941 we had contained the threat, and in 1942 the Germans did well only because they exploited Allied weaknesses off the American coast and in the Caribbean. We spent the first half of 1942 plugging those gaps. It was from the summer of 1942 onwards, when the Germans started to concentrate on the Gap again, that we needed to look carefully at the decision making; the arguments had recently been documented in Corelli Barnett's book. He still found it surprising that the potentially decisive effect was not appreciated.

Corelli Barnett himself commented on this theme. Having stressed the close co-operation that existed between the Navy and Coastal Command at the working level, he said that co-operation between the Navy and the Air Ministry was another thing altogether – there was the bitterest rivalry which came to a head in 1942 in what Dudley Pound called "the battle of the air". It was very serious, and at the time Joubert and Pound were on the same side. It was Bomber Command, backed by the Air Staff, and largely by Winston also, that caused the trouble. So there was a tremendous battle throughout 1942 over about 50 aircraft of one kind and another which the Air Staff refused to release. Jack Tovey, C-in-C Home Fleet, said he doubted if the inhabitants of Cologne would have noticed if they had been bombed by 750 aircraft rather than 1000.

Barnett then referred to the Commanders-in-Chief. No other top commander could match Harris for public relations, except for

Montgomery. None of the men at the top of Coastal Command – Bowhill, Joubert or Slessor (who had great political skills) - had quite the relentless egotistical "shove" of Harris or Monty. *Air Vice Marshal Oulton* felt that people were often unfair about Harris, who was pulled out of Washington and told to get the war going against Germany. He must have thought his task almost impossible – to do it there must be no diversions whatsoever, and we need everything we've got if we are to succeed. He must shut his eyes to everything else and do the job flat out. *Barnett* responded by quoting Harris's statement in early 1942, when he wrote to Churchill describing Coastal Command as a "a rare obstacle to victory". That was the charge against him, that he was so single-minded in fighting his corner that he missed the repercussions for the Battle of the Atlantic.

It was then suggested to *Barnett* that since the government had not worked out how much was needed to feed the country, perhaps the priorities between the Battle of the Atlantic and the Bomber Offensive had not been properly worked out. *Barnett* replied that in fact, by 1941/2/3, many economists were working on this and they did have calculations of the total tonnage of shipping required to carry it. By 1942 the tonnage coming in was falling behind what we needed so we were eating into stocks, which one could do for a time but not very long. The real worry for the War Cabinet was to see these accountancy figures. Also, the Air Staff and Bomber Command never seemed to grasp that, if the U-boat actually won, their aircraft would be grounded for lack of fuel, for it all came in tankers, and the tanker losses were relatively higher than the rest. Churchill wavered in 1942, recognising that the Battle of the Atlantic could lose us the war but also that the bomber offensive was tremendously important.

One other question related to Bomber Command also aroused much discussion. *Professor Rohwer* referred to it when expressing surprise that little effort was made to bomb the U-boat pens when under construction and vulnerable, whereas subsequent attacks succeeded only in killing French civilians. *Squadron Leader Spooner* thought the reason why the U-boat pens were not attacked at this time was fear of causing casualties among French citizens – our later attacks were more a matter of desperation. *Dr Price,* however, said that the RAF did try to bomb these Biscay ports; the problem was the same we met until the arrival of a really good escort fighter: if we bombed by day we were shot down – we didn't have long-range escorts – and by night we were not accurate enough to hit the target. *Corelli Barnett* said that in mid 1941 Joubert wrote to the Air Ministry asking if Bomber Command could bomb them while they were being built, to which CAS replied that this would be a total waste of resources and we were causing far more damage by going for the yards. *Dr Price* accepted that but asked whether, if they had tried to bomb the pens, they should have gone by day and been shot out of the sky, or by night with a three mile CEP. He did not think the outcome would have been any different.

The consequences for the local populations were also considered. *Commander Hague* recalled visiting Brest as a Midshipman in 1950: the damage was terrible – worse than in Wilhelmshaven. We were not popular; we did not exactly get spat on in the streets but we did not go out after dark. The trouble with Brest was that one could not say: "Here is the town, and over here are the U-boat pens". They were all mixed in together; it was rather like trying to hit Portsmouth dockyard without hitting Portsmouth. *Group Captain Madelin* mentioned that Harris himself contrasted the political flak which came from Dresden with the flak which did not come over Brest and Lorient and St Nazaire. He put this down to the fact that these attacks had wide support, having been requested by the Navy, supported by the RAF, and backed by the Cabinet. So everyone was for it and no-one against.

Mr Green took the discussion forward to the attacks on V1 launch sites in 1944, and the advice which had been sought from Sir William McAlpine as to the best moment to attack such targets. The answer was just after the concrete had been poured, because semi-setting concrete would be blown everywhere making reconstruction very difficult.

After *Air Vice-Marshal Gill* had pointed out that the 22,000lb Grand Slam was the only weapon capable of penetrating such targets, and the Lancaster the only aircraft capable of dropping one, *Mr Cox* said that deep penetration bombs were used from mid-1944 onwards against the pens, but that was very late in the campaign. It must be remembered that the bombs were precision engineered and in relatively short supply, as were the trained crews to drop them, so targets need to be selected carefully. Moreover by 1944 when the weapons and techniques were ready there were possible alternatives available. With the planning for OVERLORD far advanced, it had to be decided whether to deploy such precious weapons against U-Boat pens in France, which it was hoped to capture fairly quickly using ground forces, or against other high value targets such as tunnels, viaducts, or V-weapons. It again came down to the question of timing, and, whilst historians might search for rational decision-making across the board, in practice in wartime people were subjected to many conflicting pressures. Those affecting Churchill at any one point in the war were not necessarily those troubling C-in-C Coastal Command. The fog of war, *Cox* said, was such that nobody could make an entirely rational set of decisions across the board because he was not in possession of all relevant information.

Captain O'Sullivan stated that there was no record of the Navy, which should have been concerned, saying to Churchill, or anyone else, that the pens needed to be bombed before it was too late. With 20/20 hindsight they might have done so, but he agreed with Mr Cox that life was not that simple.

B) COASTAL COMMAND OPERATIONS, TECHNIQUES AND EQUIPMENT

"For most people, the Battle of the Atlantic meant getting up at some ghastly hour. going out in the pouring rain, waiting for your aircraft to be made serviceable, flying out into the Atlantic in foul weather, not seeing anything at all, and coming back 12 hours later to somewhere like Ballykelly with your heart in your mouth, missing Ben Twitch by inches. This happened not once but a thousand times for many people; for three years they would see nothing. Then, for one fleeting moment if they were lucky, they might actually see something. For many people one sighting in the whole war was better than average." Coastal Command operations were thus characterised by *AVM Oulton* as very demanding but essentially unglamorous, without the satisfaction of the prospect of much action against the enemy. Other contributors echoed this view; *ACM Stack* said that he completed two tours on Sunderlands but never found "anything but tunny boats and fishing boats". A number of speakers mentioned the strain of operations: *Wg Cdr Martin* commented upon 12hr sorties with no automatic pilot and non-existent nav. aids – the legacy he said of "antediluvian RAF equipment between the wars". *AVM Downey* said that ops were terribly tiring and he recalled that on occasions during long sorties while sharing the flying, he awoke to find his co-pilot asleep. Fatigue also affected the radar operators and gunners, and any lapses in radar or visual lookout could mean a lost U-boat sighting.

Cdr Gardner commented that one could only wonder about the alertness of crews on station after long transits in noisy and uncomfortable aircraft. Moreover, as *ACM Stack* and *Gp Capt Richardson* explained, the aircrews' working day was further extended by extensive pre- and post-flight briefings.

There was some discussion over the relative operational performance standard attained by different crews. *Sqn Ldr Laughland* singled out *Sqn Ldr Bulloch* in this respect, commenting that the latter's crew achieved 21 sightings and 5 kills at a time when most crews were seeing nothing. It was suggested that Bulloch's success owed much to the sense of enthusiasm he generated amongst his crew, and his practice of rotating radar operators to maintain lookout freshness. *AVM Oulton* thought that despite the absence of sightings all his crews remained very keen to be the next to succeed, though he did acknowledge that some crews overflew U-boats without seeing them. Crew morale appeared to remain generally high despite the long hours searching seemingly empty seas, though *AVM Downey* observed that it could fluctuate according to circumstances at the time. He cited low points caused by losses to Ju88s during the Biscay battles and by difficulties with equipment etc; conversely, the introduction of effective kit such as the Liberator enhanced morale, and perhaps surprisingly, spirits were high on the Anson sqns even though that aircraft was deemed to be "virtually useless at everything".

ACM Barraclough made the telling point that at the outbreak of war, Coastal Command's prime role was to act as the eyes of the fleet, as the Navy prepared for a second Jutland. As a consequence, many squadrons had little or no ASW training, though it soon became apparent that the U-boat would be the main enemy. Turning to training, it was generally agreed that standards varied greatly. *AVM Oulton* said that technical training was not very good, and when new kit arrived in an aircraft the current aircrew ignored it. *Sqn Ldr Burningham,* talking about sonobuoys, said that "new equipment was just thrown at us . . . our only training was on the ground". This contrasted with the experience of another contributor, who remembered being trained on ASV radar by experts from Malvern who flew with the crews. *AVM Oulton* recalled that squadron training depended largely on the squadron commander. He believed that the combination of General Recce School, Naval Training School (for navigators) and OTU was adequate preparation for operations, and, in answer to a question from Corelli Barnett, it was confirmed that Coastal

Command training lasted longer than that for Bomber Command. *ACM Stack* observed that much was learnt from publications like the Coastal Command Review, which related details of successful attacks; individual units would then embody new ideas into their own tactics.

However, despite intensive training, it was clear that operations were far from easy. *Mr Blanchard* said that up to 90% of maritime patrol aircraft failed to find the convoys they were tasked to protect; moreover, difficulties in aircraft navigation were compounded by convoys misreporting their own positions. He said that this situation was improved by the introduction of LORAN A in 1943, with ground stations in Scotland and Iceland, giving an effective 500 miles groundwave and 1500 miles skywave range. As an aside, he also mentioned that, for a short period, Coastal Command made use of the German CONSUL U-boat/Condor nav system. Making a supplementary point, *Sqn Ldr King* recalled that the first British ASW action was an attack by an RAF Anson on an RN submarine and he asked how such "blue on blue" engagements were avoided. *Air Cdre Greswell* said that RN submarines had to deploy from home waters to their patrol areas, particularly through the Bay of Biscay to the Mediterranean. The primary method to overcome attacks on friendly boats was to create sanitised rolling "carpets" along transit routes from which allied aircraft were excluded. *Air Cdre Greswell* thought that only HMS UNBEATEN was sunk by the RAF, but *Professor Rohwer* said that a Russian submarine suffered a similar fate when it strayed from a designated safe area.

It was clear that the effectiveness of Coastal Command operations could not be measured simply by the number of U-boat kills. Several commentators mentioned that the mere presence of an aircraft forced U-boats to submerge, thus significantly degrading their effectiveness. *Lt Cdr Gardner* said that if a submarine was kept down for long enough, then a convoy could get away – and one aircraft would put every U-boat down over a wide area. *AVM Oulton* commented that the appearance of an aircraft caused U-boats to crash dive, and that they could only do this three times in a 24 hour period; he also said, in reply to a question from *AM Sowrey*, that convoy morale was enormously lifted by the sight of a friendly aircraft. *AVM McKinley* confirmed that the very presence of an aircraft was a deterrent to the U-boats. *Wg Cdr Thow* asked whether crews were aware of any conflict between what might be termed "safe arrival of convoys" and "sinking of submarines". *ACM Stack* said he had never thought of it in those terms. but he acknowledged that morale went up when a sub was sunk, whereas the safe arrival of a convoy had no obvious effect. *Gp Capt Neubroch* then commented "you got a DFC if you sank a submarine, not if you merely protected a convoy". *Wg Cdr Cundy* said that crews took comfort after a long uneventful sortie from the thought that they might have kept a submarine down.

Coastal Command's ability to carry out operations depended upon the availability of aircraft. *Gp Capt Richardson* criticised what he termed "the inability of Command to place its resources where they were wanted when they were wanted". He believed that crews were sometimes tasked to fly nugatory missions in impossible conditions to pacify the Admiralty. He also commented unfavourably on serviceability and over-tasking, problems that were only remedied after an enquiry by an eminent academic – "a professor of beetles – of entymology" resulted in the introduction of planned maintenance and the adoption of sensible tasking rates.

Mr Edward Thomas enlarged on the importance of operations to counter the FW Condor threat, stressing that Churchill considered these to be vital after considerable losses in 1941. The Merchant Ship Fighter Unit (MSFU) was one response to the Condor menace, and *AVM Lyne* provided a useful brief on the unit's genesis and operations*. The depredations wrought by the Condors from August 1940 onwards demanded drastic action; land based fighters had insufficient range and there were no carriers available for convoy escort duties. So a decision was taken in December 1940 to fit catapults to selected merchant ships to allow them to launch Hurricanes. A rocket-powered catapult system was quickly trialled and installed, and the first success occurred in July 1941 when a Navy pilot shot down a Condor; the first RAF combat did not take place until May 1942. According to *AVM Lyne,* the catapult fighters made eight operational launches and achieved a kill rate per sortie of over 80%, but the real success of the MSFU came in deterring the Condors from shadowing MSFU escorted convoys. In 30 months of operations, 175 MSFU voyages were completed, 12 of the 35 catapult ships were lost and one pilot was killed. In his final comment, *AVM Lyne* stated that "I never thought that the Royal Air Force had a proper gut understanding of what was at stake on the Atlantic..."

---

* See Addendum.

There was much discussion over the techniques evolved by the Command and it was apparent that the key element was the ability, or rather the inability, of the aircrews actually to see U-boats in time to allow the prosecution of an attack. Various techniques were thus developed to give crews this vital edge, and to a large extent, these methods were dependent upon the technology available. The basic problem was how to find a U-boat in the vast expanses of the Atlantic Ocean. especially at night. *Air Cdre Greswell* outlined a number of the difficulties inherent in locating submarines at night and he described some of the ideas tried, including towed, parachute and rocket powered flares; in his view, all proved unsuccessful and only the Leigh Light showed any promise. Other contributors spoke in favour of flares. *Major Hache* felt that flares gave broader illumination for a longer period, whereas the light needed a lot of accuracy, and in certain cloud conditions could cause the pilot to lose his night vision, and this view gained qualified support from *ACM Stack,* as flares gave a bigger arc of vision. However, the mass of opinion favoured the Leigh Light. *Air Cdre Greswell* gave a graphic account of the first operational attack on a U-boat, which he carried out in June 1942 against the Luigi Torelli. A number of speakers testified to the difficulties in using the light. *Wg Cdr Cundy* emphasised the need for very accurate flying skills, bearing in mind that aircraft was descending from patrol height to 300 ft, often in very dirty weather.

The radar operator would report a contact with a bearing and range – say 30 port at 10 miles – and the aircraft would set course to intercept, using the gyro as reference. The target might be on a crossing course, requiring further adjustments, as directed by the radar operator. All this required great co-ordination between the pilot and radar operator, and he emphasised the importance of assessing the relative drift. The aim was to ensure that when the light was switched on, the U-boat should be squarely in the beam at about a mile range. *Dr Grove* confirmed that the sudden illumination by the light made it difficult for the U-boat to engage the attacking aircraft. Clearly, the Leigh Light depended upon radar to locate the U-boat, and several contributors mentioned that the U-boats could detect the radar emissions with their METOX and NAXOS-U receivers. He also alluded to some useful disinformation, supposedly from a British POW, that erroneously convinced the Germans that the attacking aircraft could home on to the emissions of the METOX equipment, resulting in many U-boat crews discontinuing its use.

Once a U-boat had been found and successfully illuminated, it had to be attacked, and there was much discussion on the question of bombing techniques. *AVM Oulton* said that the pre-war bombsight was useless, and it did not take long for practising pilots to discard it and rely on their own judgement instead, *Sqn Ldr Laughland* commented that he could not remember being given any bombing training, even when on Liberators, although as he said: "The main purpose of such an aircraft was to strike and hit a U-boat". He agreed that the prime bombsighting mechanism was the "Mark 1 Eyeball". *AVM Oulton* said that accuracy was pretty poor, but improved the lower the attack was delivered: the aim was to bracket the target with a stick of depth charges – and the depth charges had to detonate no further than 10ft from a U-boat to be sure of a kill.

AVM Oulton went on to outline some remedial measures, such as the introduction of the splash target in 1943 for bombing training, and the adoption of the Mk XIV bombsight, though he himself never trusted that particular device. *Sqn Ldr Laughland* seemed to have a little more faith in the bombsight: ". . . when the navigator saw the lines going down and coinciding with the figures he pressed the tit. The middle bomb of the six was aimed to hit the U-boat". *Wg Cdr Cundy* thought that the Low Altitude Bombsight was a valuable development, working off the autopilot, sorting out the relative drift and releasing the depth charge at the right time – supposedly. *AVM Oulton* reminded his audience that sinking U-boats was not the sole preserve of the maritime patrol aircraft. "Remember the other aircraft. In the Bay, for example, we had Mosquitos and with their cannon they were just as effective at sinking submarines as others were with their depth charges. There were the Beaufighters too". He then made a telling observation about the flexibility inherent in independent air power. "This was one of the advantages of having an independent air force – as it was, when the pressure got greater, sqns were brought in from Bomber Command. Later on we brought them in from Fighter Command".

It was generally agreed that technology was of paramount importance in Coastal Command's war. The development of radar, the means of illuminating targets at night, effective weapons, and the very long range (VLR) aircraft to carry the kit were vital to its operations. For most of the war, the Command was in competition for aircraft and equipment, particularly with Bomber Command. *Sqn Ldr Spooner* commented that the impression was that Coastal

Command was the cinderella command, tending to get what was left over from Fighter and Bomber Commands, though he did acknowledge that Sir Henry Tizard worked hard on the Command's behalf. In particular, he cited the wrangle over 10 cm radar, which was allocated first to Bomber Command – a great mistake in his view and one compounded by the loss of an H2S aircraft and the capture of the cavity magnetron at the heart of the system. The result was that by the time 10 cm radar in its maritime form – ASV Mk II – was available to Coastal Command, the Germans were well on the way to producing a detector (NAXOS-U). *Mr Blanchard* observed that a modification to the ASV Mk II misled the NAXOS kit into showing emissions in inverse ratio to the real strength, so that approaching aircraft seemed to be moving away.

Lt Cdr Hague averred that HF/DF was of more value than radar as a means of detecting U-boats, and that the Germans underestimated the importance of intercepting U-boat transmissions, and put down all the Command's successes to radar. *Lt Cdr Gardner* added that HF/DF had the advantage of being a passive sensor. *Mr Blanchard* explained that most direction finding came not from the German transmissions but from the local oscillator radiation from their receivers. The signals were weak, but there was a lack of background clutter in mid-Atlantic and the signals were of a steady and continuous nature.

The development of the Leigh Light was described in some detail by *Air Cdre Greswell*, who was involved in much of the trials worked. *Mr Archibold* alluded to delays caused by the competition with Helmore's "Turbinlite", which had been originally developed for the airborne interception of night bombers. *Air Cdre Greswell* stated that the Turbinlite would have been ineffective in the ASW role as it was a broad, unfocussed, non-steerable beam, whereas the Leigh Light was a fine beam that could be aimed by the operator. *AVM Downey* commented that even on a large aircraft like the Liberator, the substantial extra weight of the light and its location outboard of the No 4 engine gave significant handling problems.

It also took time to produce effective weapons so that, once found, U-boats could be successfully attacked. The development of powerful depth charges with accurate fusing was crucial in this regard, and *Air Cdre Greswell* outlined some of the teething troubles. The main problem concerned the hydrostatic fuse which, though effective in laboratory tests, initially failed to detonate at the correct depth in operational conditions. The problem was around the fuse, and it took some months before a fix was found. In his view, it was not until September or October 1942 that the Command had a reliable and lethal weapon, rather than July 1942 as John Terraine had claimed in his lecture.

The provision of VLR aircraft was vital to the successful prosecution of the ASW war, and a number of contributors referred to the paucity of VLR resources available, particularly the most effective of the VLR aircraft, the Liberators, which *Sqn Ldr Bulloch* called "our first real aeroplane". In his view, as few as nine of these aircraft had a disproportionate effect on the battle, notably in closing the gap in air cover south of Greenland. *Lt Cdr Gardner* observed that as late as March 1943 (the most critical stage of the U-boat war), there were only 18 VLR Liberators, though he did concede that one Liberator would put every U-boat in the area down. Ironically, once the main threat was over, resources became more plentiful. *AVM Oulton* said that for D-Day, 60 sqns of a wide variety of types were available to suppress enemy maritime activity. During the discussions on technology, *Corelli Barnett* observed that there seemed to have been a "competition between rival incompetencies in the field of technology". He said that new equipment came along so late, and on both sides the full panoply was not fully deployed until 1942/early 43 or even later. *Sqn Ldr Bulloch* agreed that technical advances on each side affected the balance of advantage: a deadly game of leap frog. He listed: "improvements in ASV radar, which was of little value before 1941; effective air-delivered depth charges, but not until 1942; no AP ammunition, but devastatingly effective steel-headed RPs." *Corelli Barnett* then made a very important general point over equipment: "We were supposed to be a sea power, dependent on sea communications, yet how critically dependent we were on US kit of every description – the Liberator. the Hudson, Canadian-built escorts, US-built escort carriers, a lot of help over radar/radar components. As a maritime power we could not provide the kit we needed". *AVM Oulton* agreed that we did not have the resources to satisfy our needs, and *Sqn Ldr Burningham* added aviation spirit to the list of essential supplies that came from the USA. *Dr Price* mentioned that left to our own resources we only had the capacity to produce around 100 cavity magnetons, hence the vital contribution of US mass production. *Corelli Barnett* returned to the mismatch between Britain's strategic equipment needs and the country's ability to satisfy these requirements. He believed that a peacetime export-led economy was ill-suited to wartime conditions and he brought the discussions full circle by wondering what combined naval/air effort would be needed to protect our vital imports today.

C) INTELLIGENCE

AVM Betts asked whether the British and German authorities were aware of the extent to which their cryptographic activities had been compromised,

Professor Rohwer explained that, though the German authorities knew that the British were obtaining valuable intelligence information, compromise of the German naval codes was not thought to be the source. Döenitz suspected that the leaks came from other communications, because, although it was known that the British had captured an Enigma machine, it was thought to be useless without access to the daily settings. On occasion the British gained these settings from captured vessels, but it was more often due to the work of the cryptanalysts at Bletchley Park. On the German side, British cyphers had been broken before the war. There was a brief pause when the codes were changed in August 1940, but the traffic was soon being read once more.

Professor Rohwer gave examples of the successes achieved by the cryptanalysts In particular he restated his view that the re-routeing of convoys as a result of Ultra intercepts saved more than 300 ships. He also made reference to the problems caused for the British when technical improvements to the Enigma resulted in temporary Ultra "blackouts", as in early 1943 when sinkings rose dramatically during a period when the codes were not being read.

Professor Rohwer also referred to the period before the USA officially entered the war, when the British supplied Ultra intelligence to the Americans from 1 September 1941 onwards. He stated that the USN had attempted to intercept the ADMIRAL SCHEER in November 1941, and he believed that, had the attempt succeeded, it would certainly have precipitated US entry into the war before Pearl Harbor.

He went on to say that Döenitz was so enraged by the fact that the British frequently transmitted accurate plots of U-boats – information ironically gained from German decrypts of British codes – that he sought to stem the leaks; even to the extent of having himself investigated as a possible source. The great mistake made by the Germans, however, was to allow the cryptanalysts to undertake the investigation into how the Admiralty was gaining its intelligence. Because these men had such unshakeable faith in Enigma, and indeed considered it unbreakable in a timescale which would produce useful intelligence, they suspected other sources, and especially radar. The Germans were also unaware of the importance of HF/DF in determining U-boat dispositions and were not aware of the extent to which their use of weather codes assisted the British analysts.

Dr Eric Grove pointed out that the US Navy's Admiral Simms had revealed in his book on the First World War, "Victory at Sea", that one of the main advantages of convoy was the opportunities it afforded for the exploitation of Sigint by evasive routeing. He doubted, however, if the Germans had ever read the book. In addition the Döenitz system was so dependant on secure radio communications that it would not have been able to function without it.

AVM Betts then asked about the efficacy of the severe restrictions placed on radio transmissions from RAF maritime patrol aircraft. *Professor Rohwer* said that, despite these restrictions useful fixes were obtained on signals from VLR aircraft. *Air Cdre Greswell* said that one exception to the restrictions was the "Flash" attack report. *Professor Rohwer* said that U-boats were also very conscious of the danger of revealing their positions, and late in the war a burst-transmission facility had been developed to counter this threat. *Professor Rohwer* also revealed that British intelligence had a better understanding of the effectiveness of German acoustic torpedoes than the Kriegsmarine themselves. This was because they were reading the German reports on the subiect, and were then able to compare them with their own observations. In this way they knew that the U-boat captains were unaware that a high proportion of the torpedoes were exploding harmlessly in the target's wake.

Edward Thomas, in reply to a question on the balance between the use of Ultra and technological and operational factors, stated that Ultra's contribution varied, and that it was difficult to know exactly where the balance between factors lay. He thought that Ultra's contribution towards saving shipping in 1941 was crucial because in that year there was something of a lull, and Britain was able to build up something of a surplus balance sheet, particularly in regard to merchant ship construction. He believed that all that really ensured Britain's survival took place in 1941. By 1943 Ultra was playing second fiddle to the operational forces, lt helped such forces as we had, which were increasing in numbers and capability, but one of its most important contributions was in evasive routeing. In the end, however, unless someone dropped a depth charge in the right place, all the Ultra in the world could not help.

Gp Capt Richardson agreed with *Mr Thomas*. He had been commanding 502 Squadron flying Whitleys from Limavady and St Eval. Although the aircraft would be given information on where to find U-Boats on passage in the Bay of Biscay they seldom turned out to be where they were expected. In 1941, however good the information from Ultra it was never quite good enough to concentrate the air effort where it was required. He stated that in his experience it was very difficult to find anything and his squadron had very little success. He also went on to say that security concerning Ultra was tight, and they never received any information on sources whatsoever. They thought that somebody was sitting overlooking the U-Boat pens.

Mr Thomas replied that SOE did not provide intelligence on U-Boats. There was an MI6 agent at Lorient, but the only real intelligence came from Ultra. In 1941 when the U-Boats sailed from their Biscay bases they would be accompanied by a minesweeper which would signal that such and such a U-boat had slipped. British intelligence therefore knew when a U-Boat sailed, but it was not known where they were until Döenitz signalled its patrol area later.

D) MARITIME/AIR DOCTRINE AND POLICY

Neither Service pre-war had appreciated the extent of the U-boat threat or of its technical challenge. The Admiralty was over-confident about the combined effectiveness of ASDIC in surface ships supported by carrier-borne aircraft. Convoys were considered unnecessary unless unrestricted submarine warfare developed; according to *Dr Grove* and *Captain O'Sullivan* there were no pre-war exercises in convoy protection or realistic training in the use of ASDIC. RAF doctrine offered no alternative; moving ships in convoy simply provided large and easy targets for attack from the air. But was there culpable complacency? Several speakers mentioned the speed at which the threat from Germany developed, revolutionising the strategic background to British military planning. Until well into the thirties RN priorities were Imperial rather than European. Japan was the most likely enemy, which implied battlefleet actions – not attritional campaigns in defence of trade. Even when a threat from Germany developed, neither its high-seas fleet nor its U-boats were so numerous that to contain them mainly in the North Sea – achieved in World War I, as *Dr Willmott* pointed out – seemed out of the question. For the RAF, for reasons of domestic politics as well as Air Staff doctrine, air defence and the building of a large bomber force received most attention and resources. What drastically altered the strategic picture was the invasion of Norway, followed by the fall of France. The whole western seaboard, from Biscay to North Norway became available to the German Navy. "No military planner could have foreseen such a catastrophe" *(Dr Grove)*. "The Coastal Command I joined had the wrong aircraft in the wrong place: Ansons based at stations along the East coast" *(Mr Spooner)*.

The transfer of the Fleet Air Arm from the RAF to the Navy in 1937 was not the best prelude to inter-service co-operation. Moreover, as *John Terraine* said, ideally a Supreme Commander Atlantic was called for when the USA entered the war. As it was, RN/RAF co-operation worked well enough for most of the campaign. "You have to be fairly senior before there is quarrel between the services; at working level people got on well" *(AVM Downey)*. More than one speaker paid tribute to the RN liaison team and Captain Peyton-Ward at Coastal Command HQ at Northwood. Maritime expertise was not lacking there; the C-in-C at the outbreak of war, Air Marshal Bowhill, and some of his staff officers had begun their careers in the Royal Navy.

Defining the aim of the campaign was easy enough: to get sufficient supplies through to enable the UK to feed its people and defend its territory. How best to achieve the aim proved to an unnecessary extent a painful learning process. Despite WWI experience convoys were not organised on a large enough scale. Too many ships sailed independently and, however carefully routed, were highly vulnerable unless they could steam at a minimum 20 knots. Escorts were in short supply in the early days and under-protected convoys were thought to be worse than useless; it was soon realised, said *Captain O'Sullivan*, that they were better than nothing; just as it was that if a convoy under attack scattered, the wolves could more easily devour the sheep. Better to stick together. As these lessons were learned so successes were achieved, both in shipping losses reduced and U-boats destroyed. The great U-boat aces of the first months of the war were all sunk in 1941 by surface vessels escorting convoys *(Dr Grove)*. Determining the argument about convoys and how best to protect them was that much easier when the discipline of Operational Research was brought to bear *(Sir John Barraclough)*. By 1943 the case was overwhelming but especially when aircraft and surface escorts were co-operating. Once the mid-Atlantic gap had been closed by VLR aircraft the system was complete. The U-boats eventually broke themselves on strong convoy defences.

Surprisingly, the US Navy was slow to institute a convoy system off the eastern American seaboard, with the personality of Admiral King – Anglophobe and obstinate – one of the obstacles. According to *Lt Cdr Hague*, an impassioned outburst to his face by a relatively junior RN officer may have influenced King to change his mind, but not before the U-boats had a second 'happy time' (the first being in 1940) off the American coast. Even so, the USN never formally changed its priorities for U-boat warfare: No. 1 was 'Offensive Action', with 'Safe Arrival of Convoy' low on the list. Yet, said *Hague*, "the convoy was a honey pot. Sit and wait, and they'll come".

Could the U-boat offensive have succeeded? A major problem for Germany lay in determining the amount of imports necessary for Britain to continue the war *(Herr Neitze)*. According to *Wg Cdr Broadbent*, British pre-war estimates proved much exaggerated; a requirement of 47 million tons a year was later scaled down to 26 million. More was needed once the USA was engaged and re-entry into Europe became a practical objective. With the additional resources of the USN and massively increased availability of merchant shipping when Liberty ship production came on stream the need was amply met. In the continuous and fluctuating battles at sea the ratio of U-boat successes and losses was reflected in the hopes and fears of the contestants but the judgment of one syndicate member *(Major Kemp)* was that Admiral Döenitz was never in a position to have sufficient U-boats on station to break the UK lifeline. At no time, however, was it possible for Britain and her Allies to relax. This was one campaign that lasted from September 1939 to May 1945 and had to be won, not by a last and final battle but progressively as the war developed.

E) GERMAN OPERATIONS AND EQUIPMENT

The point made by *Lieutenant-Commander Wilson* was fundamental to the whole battle against the U-boats – German Naval planners had not anticipated going to war until 1944. As a result U-boat Command was, from the point of view of numbers, as unprepared as the Allies. But training was given the highest priority as *Lieutenant-Commanders Hague* and *Gardner* emphasized. A submarine was required to carry out sixty six attacks whilst working-up in the Baltic and pre-war crews' training was personally supervised by Dönitz. The nine months of hard slog before a U-boat was passed fit for patrol compared very favourably with the few weeks allotted to British ships and submarines and was continued at a time when heavy losses brought a great strain on the U-boat recruitment programme. As in World War One some commanding officers were sent on their first patrol without previous submarine operational experience. Some of these lasted less than a month in the North Atlantic.

The policy which Dönitz evolved required frequent signals from submarines on patrol so that shore control could dictate the strategic dispositions of the boats at sea. As *Flight-Lieutenant Aveyard* pointed out the Germans did not realise the extent to which these communications were being intercepted. The submarines' signals provided directional fixes for both shore stations and ships fitted with High Frequency Direction Finding (HFDF) equipment as well as providing valuable information via the Ultra decryption organisation.

The comparison between the staffs involved was emphasized by *Dr. Alfred Price*. From one of Dönitz's senior staff officers he had learned of the operational staff structure of U-boat Command – a few senior staff supported by a small number of highly qualified U-boat C.Os. Each day the staff would discuss and, if need be, argue with their admiral over the conduct of the convoy battle. This discussion was greatly aided by Dönitz's rule of seeing all C.Os on return from patrol – a fount of immediate operational experience which was very similar to that available from the Allied escort C.Os when interviewed by C-in-C Western Approaches.

Over the early years of the war, as U-boat numbers increased, there were definite methods of operation adopted by the U-boats as *Lieutenant-Commander Hague* pointed out. The ideal approach was downwind on the surface, a heavy Atlantic sea and swell on the beam making the boat hard to handle, while a head sea cut down the approach speed. On a clear night it was preferable to put the convoy up-moon but each C.O. with growing experience, developed his own pattern of attack. Some preferred to enter the convoy prior to firing, others to attack the fringes. When angled torpedoes were introduced the task was greatly eased at ranges of 500-600 yards. If attacking from the bow at speeds up to sixteen knots the time in the convoy was very brief and it was preferable to remain on the surface when withdrawing. An alternative method, more hair-raising and less efficient, was to dive ahead of the convoy, allow it to overrun the U-boat and fire from submerged. With convoy speeds of seven and a half to nine knots and a U-boat's maximum dived speed for a short period no more than eight to nine knots, the time available for an attack was limited. The tremendous noise in the water made it virtually impossible to identify individual merchant ships and an attack from periscope depth on a dark night was fraught with peril. The delay of twenty minutes or more required to reload torpedoes made it virtually impossible to engage for a second time while dived although some well-drilled boats contrived it during a surface attack.

During the withdrawal at night the presence of an aircraft fitted with centimetric radar could be disastrous for a submarine which had failed to detect the radar transmissions. If the aircraft were fitted with a Leigh Light an attack could be instantaneous – if not the pouncer astern of the convoy could be a major threat when summoned.

The effect of aircraft on the convoy battle was decisive and acknowledged as such by the Germans. A submarine C.O had little or no evidence as to whether he had been sighted or detected should an aircraft appear while he was on the surface. Unless otherwise ordered he had to dive, reducing his speed dramatically and cutting his range of vision to only a couple of miles. From late 1942 onwards detection by an aircraft could bring further retribution – the Allied Support Group. This was a force of escorts separate from the convoy's close escort which engaged submarines well beyond the convoy area. Their duty was not 'the safe and timely arrival' of the merchant ships but the destruction of submarines. They would hunt to exhaustion, in one case for over forty hours.

Lieutenant-Commander Hague answered questions on the replenishment of U-boats while at sea. In areas other than the North Atlantic, rendezvous were arranged with merchant supply ships the majority of which were disposed of in 1941 thanks to information gained from Ultra decryptions and other intelligence, all suitably disguised as part of the hunt for Bismarck's support vessels.

An apparently less vulnerable supply line consisted of large converted submarines followed by the ten bespoke re-supply boats, known generally as 'Milch Cows' The principle was excellent and many U-boats received fuel, stores and torpedoes from the 'Milch Cows' but again Ultra decryptions exposed their whereabouts. Eventually all were sunk, the US Navy having a highly successful period in the Central Atlantic in 1943. When great reliance was placed on re-supply and the 'Milch Cow' had been sunk a major problem was posed to U-boat Command. On one occasion seven U-boats were left with minimal fuel and had to be helped by other boats transferring small quantities from their own dwindling supplies of diesel oil. As *Lieutenant-Commander Gardner* pointed out, fuel was always the critical item.

The value of aircraft in anti-submarine operations had been recognised in World War One but by 1939 insufficient preparations had been made for effective long-range patrols by the British Coastal Command. *Professor Rohwer* and others explained that the mid-Atlantic gap which was beyond the range of maritime patrol aircraft from Britain, Canada or Iceland could not be covered from bases in Greenland due to problems of weather, navigation and terrain. The gap was not adequately covered until ship-borne aircraft and the Very Long Range Liberators became available.

The German long-range aircraft, the FW200 Condor had very different tasks – reconnaissance of and attacks on merchant ships. Converted from a pre-war civilian design the Condor had navigational problems which limited its use for reconnaissance but the greatest impediment to the use of these Luftwaffe aircraft for naval support was Goering. It was not until January 1941 that Dönitz, with the Reichsmarshal away hunting, contrived to obtain operational control of KG40, the group of Condors based at Bordeaux. These aircraft achieved their greatest successes against single ships sailing independently – there were frequently too many guns in a convoy to allow an uninterrupted bombing run. However the convoys to and from Gibraltar did suffer from time to time – HG53 was attacked by nine Condors following a U-boat sighting of the convoy. As the convoy operations moved further into the Atlantic and Allied air superiority in the Biscay area was established these aircraft became of marginal value.

Answering a query from his Chairman about German operations against Coastal Command, *Professor Rohwer* said that there were some attacks on British bases up to June 1941 but, with the invasion of Russia, the Luftwaffe was too hard pressed to intervene effectively in the U-boat war. There were also initial attempts to dominate the Biscay area with long-range fighters but the Beaufighters and Mosquitos soon established an effective superiority over the limited number of aircraft available. This was fortunate for the Allies at a time when the Henschel 293 guided bombs were achieving success against support groups and convoys off Biscay. HMS Egret, a sloop, was sunk and other ships damaged during attacks by He 177 and Do 217 aircraft.

Another form of aircraft support was the limited use of towed rotor-craft in the South Atlantic and Indian Oceans in 1942. This method of increasing the submarine's horizon had little success and presented several operational penalties, not least of which was the inevitable loss of craft and pilot should the submarine be forced to dive. True helicopters were used in the Aegean in 1942-3, flying from a captured Yugoslav aviation support ship but neither of these means of reconnaissance was used in the North Atlantic.

Prompted by *Squadron Leader Grimston's* questions *Professor Rohwer* spoke of German submarine developments during the war. The Walter closed-cycle diesel using High Test Peroxide (HTP) could propel a submarine at twenty knots for limited periods. Some test boats were constructed and, though a fleet of 300 was projected in 1944, construction and fuel difficulties prevented implementation of the plan. Development was concentrated on what became the Types XXI and XXIII, diesel electric boats of high performance capable (Type XXI) of fifteen knots dived. The first of these became operational just before the end of the war, too late to affect the outcome.

11. Lessons for the Present

Air Marshal Sir John Curtiss

I have been asked to reflect on the wartime experiences we have heard about today in relation to post-war developments and to give my views on why we did not have to re-learn all the lessons of World War Two all over again. I shall also show how these experiences related to the Falklands Campaign in 1982. I am not sure, incidentally, if the fact that I never served in Coastal Command is the reason for my being asked to conclude this seminar. However, I did get first-hand experience of the Battle, first in August 1940 when I crossed to Canada in a fast two-ships passage, and again in 1942 on returning from New Zealand.

Having fought a battle of the Atlantic in World War I which we had barely won we found ourselves facing a far worse peril in 1939, singularly ill equipped and particularly in the air. As John Terraine has pointed out, it took some two years to re-learn most of the lessons and to re-equip our maritime forces. That this did not happen again following World War Two was almost entirely due to the fact that before we had time to fully disarm we were faced with a new enemy with rapidly developing and even more formidable equipment, and by 1948 we were engaged in a new war, albeit a "cold war" rather than a hot one. What is more, the threats were rapidly changing and maritime forces were faced with new and even more deadly types of submarine: first the cruise missile, anti-shipping submarine, and then - following the advent of the nuclear submarine - the submarine-launched ballistic missile version. And now the Cold War has ended - more dramatically and suddenly than we could ever have expected.

Thus, within a comparatively short while from the ending of the Second World War, the maritime forces were faced with a very much more serious and difficult threat. However, it is somewhat ironic that although this new threat was more difficult to find and follow it was plainly visible in a political sense, so resources were found to develop counter measures and a great deal of effort was expended in detecting and trailing Soviet submarines - and particularly the ballistic missile firing variety - to their operating areas off the American coast. These Cold War threats required a NATO-wide approach and close co-operation between navies and maritime air. NATO maritime forces shared their expertise and their information and furthermore exercised together frequently. RAF maritime crews thus operated and trained worldwide and not only with NATO nations; they also carried out annual exercises and competitions with Australian and New Zealand maritime forces, thus gaining an immense amount of experience of worldwide operations against a variety of targets in a wide range of environments.

It must be said that the new threats I have mentioned did not reduce the other roles traditionally held by the maritime air forces such as long range maritime reconnaissance, communications and search and rescue. If anything, with the advent of new and better equipment, these requirements assumed greater importance as the maritime aircrews were able to do more and do it better. In the event of a shooting war one of the major roles for the Allied maritime forces was to help clear a path for the Allied Strike Carrier Force into its operational areas off the Norwegian coast. This task would require all the roles of the LRMP to be exercised.

In consequence by the time 1982 came along No 18 Group possessed 32 Nimrod K 2s, maximised for ASW but also adept at maritime reconnaissance and search and rescue. We also had a small number of Sea King helicopters which were to play a limited role in Ascension and after the war in the Falklands. The Buccaneer anti-shipping squadrons were never employed. The Nimrod crews' ASW expertise was long honed in stalking Soviet submarines transiting through the Greenland, Iceland and Faroes Gaps and they were second to none. The development of new under-water sensors, sonobuoys, and on-board signal processing and computing equipment made the Nimrod Mk2 first among equals with the Lockheed P3 - but it was not their ASW expertise that was to be called upon for the Falklands campaign.

Fortunately the aircraft had been equipped with the new Thorn EMI Searchwater radar capable of long-range detection of shipping and of producing course, speed, length and even the profile of the shipping displayed - no doubt the best maritime radar in the business. The Nimrod's maritime reconnaissance capabilities were to be tested to the full and Searchwater was the most used piece of equipment. It must be said, however, that some further experience and development of its more sophisticated capabilities were still required by the start of the campaign, and its operation during the war was not wholly without problems.

The Falklands was, of course, another of those wars we were never going to have to fight and one for which absolutely no planning had been done. After all who could have supposed that the United Kingdom, on its own, would launch an invasion fleet across 8000 miles of ocean against an enemy operating off its own doorstep? It was enough to give any politician apoplexy if he even considered such a bizarre idea. That it succeeded in such an overwhelming and dramatic fashion, with minimum loss of life, says a very great deal about qualities and the capabilities of the British Armed Forces. Mind you, had we not been blessed with a Prime Minister equipped with sheer bloody-minded determination it could not have happened at all; Galtieri would still be in power, the Falklands would have remained the Malvinas forever, and we would have sent entirely the wrong signal to all like-minded tyrants. Sadly Saddam Hussein was demonstrably deaf and blind.

Reverting to World War Two, one of the major lessons learnt was that Royal Navy/Royal Air Force co-operation was absolutely essential if the submarine was to be successfully prosecuted, and in the fire and flame of the Battle of the Atlantic a new spirit of co-operation was forged. The fact that the air sank as many submarines as the surface forces was a great help in this respect and showed conclusively that the one could not succeed without the other. Nor was the lesson forgotten after the war. Indeed in 1965 or thereabouts C-in-C Fleet moved his Headquarters to Northwood so as to sit alongside C-in-C Coastal Command and thus continue their excellent co-operation in the new scenarios of the Cold War. So it was that in April 1982 when the Falklands crisis arose the two Command Headquarters had worked alongside each other for many years in both their national and their NATO hats. I, as AOC 18 Group – as Coastal Command had by now become – had worked closely with Admiral Sir John Fieldhouse for over a year and we got along extremely well, as did our respective staffs. It was therefore a fairly obvious move when I was appointed Air Commander to the Task Force at a very early stage.

At that time it was not envisaged that the RAF's participation would exceed our maritime patrol aircraft but before very long the

18 Group Order of Battle included all those air assets proceeding south of Ascension Island. Only the transport force, except when operating south to supply the Task Force, was controlled centrally by the Ministry of Defence, and the RAF's Harrier squadron embarked in HMS HERMES was under Sandy Woodward, the commander of the Task Group.

In many ways it was extremely fortunate that my own career had spanned all the major Commands and I had served operationally in Bomber, Transport and Fighter Commands. As an aside, I have always been very critical of the over-specialisation in GD officers' careers, albeit for the best of economic reasons, and it soon became quite plain that my staff officers who had spent their lives exclusively in one role had some difficulty in appreciating the unique requirements of the different assets at our disposal. However, the exception always proves the rule and my Chief of Staff, AVM George Chesworth, known in the Group as "Mr Nimrod" and who had served in every rank at Kinloss, was absolutely invaluable to me throughout and proved of critical importance in providing on the spot advice over the very difficult first Vulcan operations from Ascension Island.

So before the war was over I had added to my staff officers with Harrier, Vulcan, Hercules, Chinook, land/air warfare and logistics expertise. They provided an excellent and cohesive staff who worked well with their Naval opposite numbers in very crowded circumstances. The new ops room had not then been completed and for obvious reasons we could not take over the NATO accommodation. As an ex-Commandant and DS of this great establishment here I have to say that the Bracknell trained officers stood out from their fellows.

As an unforeseen, unplanned operation we really had to make it up as we went along – there were few if any precedents to go by but the age-old principles of war and good sound planning procedures stood us in good stead. It has to be said that although it was very hard work, involving very long hours, it was tremendous fun and carried out in great good humour by a few staff who all appreciated each others' expertise. That does not mean that we did not appreciate the difficulties that faced us or that there were not very many potential dangers that could turn the operation very sour indeed. But I have always found that in peace or war – and however difficult and serious the position may be – a sense of humour is a tremendous help all round.

But one thing above all is certain: the Falklands campaign demonstrated once and for all, to even the greatest sceptic, the flexibility of air power. Let me give you an example. A RAFG Harrier squadron, based in Central Europe in the close air support role, was within three weeks deck and flight refuelling trained, and equipped with Sidewinder missiles in case it was needed in the air defence role. In the end it was not required but the rapidity with which roles could be altered and assets switched and deployed long distances was truly astonishing. Mind you the rules had changed and all the peacetime restraints and bureaucracy had been swept away. As one senior officer put it, the civil servants were hammered into the woodwork for the duration. Here I should like to pay a particular tribute to the aerospace industry; they were able to come up with almost every modification asked for and did it in double quick time.

The key to the whole of the RAF's participation was of course flight refuelling. At the beginning of the campaign none of the RAF's aircraft that were to be deployed were capable on in-flight refuelling, but in extremely short order Harriers, Vulcans, Nimrods and Hercules had been so equipped and all were operating when required all the way to the Falklands. But flexibility went further than that; Vulcan crews that had never been trained in low-level conventional bombing were soon trained in that capability as were Nimrod crews. Sqn Ldr Bulloch will be interested to know that apart from some markings on the view screen the Nimrod had no bomb sight either. The Vulcan was also equipped with anti-radar missiles and dropped two in anger. The new Stingray torpedo was rushed into service and the Nimrod was also equipped with the Harpoon anti-shipping missile, SLIR, PNGs, and even Sidewinder missiles.

You may wonder at the Nimrod being equipped with iron bombs but a number of Argentine merchant ships kept appearing in the vicinity of the Ascension Island and we wanted to deter them if necessary from coming too close. As to the Nimrod fighter, this came about because one of our aircraft on a long-range patrol ahead of the Task Force had stumbled across the Argentine 707 that had been acting as their long-range reconnaissance aircraft and reporting the progress and composition of the fleet. It had always kept outside surface-to-air missile range and I conceived the somewhat wild idea of fitting the Nimrod with air-to-air missiles. Somewhat to my surprise the idea was accepted but inevitably no further interception ever occurred.

At the start of the operation, however, we had none of these goodies and it seemed that all we would be able to do was escort the Task Force and provide maritime reconnaissance out to about 1800 miles from Ascension. The Falkland Islands were some 3500 miles away.

Another point that needs emphasising was our lack of intelligence about Argentina's armed forces. In the understandable economies of peacetime there was hardly any intelligence effort available to devote to that part of the world. We therefore had to rely upon Jane's Fighting Ships and All the World's Aircraft. Certainly the Argentine Navy seemed on paper to be most formidable, equipped with some British Type 42 destroyers and a fixed wing aircraft carrier. Their Commander in Chief, Admiral Anaya, was by far the most bellicose of Galtieri's top brass, at least until the shooting started. We also had very little better information about the Islands we were seeking to recover.

I must from the start establish the vital importance and the drawbacks of Ascension Island. It was vital for all our operations in the South Atlantic and a very important staging and supply point for the RN. In the speed with which the Task Force had been assembled and despatched south from the UK it had been impossible to load the fleet and its supply train tactically. This was all done off Ascension Island using helicopters especially flown in for the purpose. Some of the RN Harriers and the RAF aircraft were not ready to board before the Task Force left the UK and they were flown to Ascension to be loaded on HERMES and ATLANTIC CONVEYOR.

Unfortunately Ascension possessed but one runway, albeit a good one which had been built by the USAF for flights down range from its missile testing facilities at Cape Kennedy. It also had very limited hard standings or parking areas available and aircraft could not be parked off these areas nor helicopters landed, as the whole of the island consisted of volcanic rock and dust. The maximum parking places available never exceeded 21 and when you understand that it could require up to 17 tankers to get Nimrods, Vulcans or Hercules down and back to their operating areas you have some idea of the problem and the need for continued juggling of assets to meet the priorities of the time. In addition helicopters for search and rescue, and Harriers and then Phantoms for air defence were required. In consequence Vulcans,

Nimrods and Hercules had to be redeployed to holding airfields at Gibraltar and in the UK as the various priorities of employment of our air assets changed.

The first operational sortie we were asked to run was recce of the South Georgia Islands ahead of the task group detailed to retake them, to see if there were any signs of Argentine surface ships and where the major icebergs were located. As the Nimrod was not yet equipped with AAR the Victor tankers were the only aircraft capable of undertaking the task. So once again crews were asked to take on roles for which they had never trained and did so successfully.

So in the early days of the campaign our task was to sweep the ocean ahead of the Task Force watching for any Argentine naval or merchant ships and keeping an eye out for Russian AGIs who soon came to sit off Ascension for the duration. In addition, because Ascension Island had become such an essential hub for all our operations, it seemed reasonable that the Argentines might try to inhibit our use in some way so constant patrols had to be flown around the island to spot Argentine shipping, and later on we installed radar and fighters in case of any air attack. It would have taken very little to put us out of operation.

In the early days our maximum range, which allowed no time on station, was 1800 miles from Ascension; the Falkland Islands still lay a further 1700 miles south. However, just 32 days after the Argentine invasion our first air-to-air refuelling Nimrod was available for operations and given the tankers we could now reach the Argentine coastline and the Falklands themselves. This was a perfect example of the ingenuity and speed of our industry and our engineers and if the modification could only be described as Heath Robinson in concept, it was easy to incorporate and worked without any mishaps. An ex-Vulcan probe was inserted above and behind the pilots' cabin, and ordinary bowser hose was then run down from the probe and along the cabin floor past the navigators and the acoustic team to exit just aft of the main cabin into the No 7 tank. Needless to say since the war the installation has been considerably cleaned up.

Now equipped with the modified Nimrods we were able to extend our operations considerably, always provided that tanker assets were available, and once the Task Force had reached its operating areas off the Islands the main task of the maritime air was to assist the patrolling nuclear submarines to watch for the Argentine Fleet and see if they were going to come out and give battle. So for the remainder of the campaign the Nimrod crews were able to provide reconnaissance around and ahead of the Fleet, radar and visual reconnaissance of the Argentine coast in conjunction with the SSNs, mail drops to surface vessels, and search and rescue for a number of operations.

Even when priorities called for a Vulcan sortie the Nimrod had an important part to play in assisting the Vulcan make its first vital tanker rendezvous after leaving the target. Once again the Searchwater radar and its electronic countermeasures suite proved invaluable. No RV was ever missed although as you know one Vulcan broke its probe in turbulent conditions and had to divert to Rio de Janciro where the crew were hospitably entertained having been put in charge of one of Brazil's Bracknell-trained officers.

The Argentine Navy possessed two German-built diesel electric submarines and although the Nimrod could do nothing to help having no time on task off the Falklands they did pose a real threat to the Task Force. Whether they actually came out is difficult to determine although we heard that they were having difficulties with their torpedo firing equipment and with their periscopes. Inevitably some of the local whales had a pretty lean time.

Priorities for the employment of the air assets were decided by the FLAIRGO (Flag Air and General Officers Committee) that met once or twice a day under the C-in-C. We had to make our minds up two or three days in advance so that we could juggle our resources accordingly. Because of the pen space I have already referred to and the number of tankers available we could only run one bomber long-range maritime patrol at any one time. We could get a Hercules down to the Task Force in addition as long as it was a straight there and back affair, but some of those sorties took up to 28 hours.

One operation that we planned and executed and which gave me considerable concern was reinforcing the Task Force with four Harriers before the final assault. This required the aircraft, all from No 1 Squadron, to fly in pairs non-stop from Ascension Island, escorted only by their tankers, to land on board HMS HERMES lying off the Falklands. The RN thought we were foolhardy, but the pilots involved showed no apparent concern and the operation worked perfectly. The aircraft were much needed in the theatre.

The longest LRMP sortie took $19\frac{1}{2}$ hours but none saw anything more exciting than a large number of fishing boats. However, negative information in such a situation can be equally valuable and meant that the RN carriers did not have to expose themselves to the threat of Exocets in order to confront the

Argentine Fleet. We did not know it at the time but from the moment the BELGRANO was sunk they never put their noses out of port again.

A number of even quite intelligent people have failed to understand the raison d'etre and the expenditure of much effort in the Vulcan attacks against Port Stanley airfield. Our greatest concern during the whole campaign was the preservation of the carriers and of the small number of Harriers which constituted the only air defence of the Fleet – apart from missiles – and the only air support for our land forces. At the same time the only resupply capability that the enemy had was the one runway at Port Stanley. Inevitably, the RN sent some of their Harriers against it and even tried naval bombardment. But the Argies also had some land-based Exocets nearby and these ships were then very vulnerable; indeed one of the DLGs was nearly sunk by an Exocet whilst carrying out naval bombardment. Port Stanley airfield was also well defended by anti-aircraft artillery and missiles and Sea Harriers were very vulnerable carrying out attacks for which they were neither properly equipped nor trained; one RAF officer flying with the Navy was shot down by a missile from Port Stanley and other aircraft were damaged by AA fire. None of these Harrier attacks caused any noticeable damage to the airfield.

We also wanted to send a message to the Argentines, that if necessary we could bomb the Argentine itself. This message was well received: after the first Vulcan raid they withdrew their only Mirage III squadrons to defend Buenos Aires and their attacks against the fleet during and after the landings went unescorted. You can imagine the additional problem if they had been able to run top cover against the Sea Harriers during those raids.

We also used the Vulcan equipped with the American Shrike anti-radar missile to try and put out the main Argentine radar, which was able to keep track of the Task Force throughout the landing and afterwards. The final Vulcan raid was designed to knock out any remaining Pucaras, so as to prevent them taking part when the Army captured Port Stanley. All the bombs that night were fitted with air-burst fusing.

What lessons can we learn for the future? The first must be that, however few your resources, you must never give up a capability that has a global application. I cannot imagine that we would ever consign flight refuelling to the scrap heap but there may be other less obvious capabilities which once given up are both hard and expensive to develop.

The next is that submarines will go on getting more difficult to detect and we must go on developing new airborne sensors and weapons to combat them, even with the Cold War seemingly over.

Then again time spent in reconnaissance is never wasted – an old adage, that no one should ever forget. Whilst the RAF could do maritime reconnaissance we had no over-the-Islands capability. Despite constant requests we never obtained any damage assessments or other information on Port Stanley airfield, and yet Sea Harrier sorties were wasted throwing bombs ineffectively at the runway. I sometimes think that the Nelson blind eye tradition can be a big handicap.

Furthermore, while staff courses can ameliorate the problem, we must try to avoid over-specialisation. You can be in danger of losing some of the inherent flexibility of air power if senior officers do not have some multi-role experience.

But at the end of the day our greatest asset was undoubtedly the very high standards of training enjoyed by the professional soldiers, sailors and airmen who fought in the Falklands. Our men are second to none and our recruiting and training policies and the rewards for service should never forget that.

12. Closing Remarks

Air Marshal Sir Frederick Sowrey Chairman the RAF Historical Society

Hindsight is a wonderful thing, given to us all by the passage of years. We must be careful that as we look at the shortcomings of 50 years ago we realise that the decisions made at the time were the best available on the information available to those who had to take them. The bottom line is that those who fought the battle on both sides did so to the best of their very considerable ability. Since 1945 a constant change has been the Air Force's form of stability. Sir John Curtiss has shown why the hiatus between the wars has not recurred since the end of the Second World War. With the ending of the Soviet threat we must perhaps look forward in the future to much more critical analysis of the circumstances that are going to arise in political terms if we do not miss the continued improvement which our forces showed in the Falklands and the Gulf War as proof of their professionalism.

Sir John Barraclough has been most complimentary about the RAF Historical Society. It is a Committee organization, for which today we owe a great deal to Air Commodore Henry Probert. We owe a considerable vote of thanks to our speakers, all of whom have given their time and ability without stint. We owe a great debt to the RAF Staff College; their organization underpins and makes possible a day like today. Lastly, Shell UK, through the good offices of one of our committee members, Tony Richardson, has offered a major contribution towards the publishing of the proceedings of today's event. This is a marvellous gesture, which will enable us to produce a slim volume similar to that for the Battle of Britain seminar, which will go to all our members, to all today's speakers, and to the Staff College.

Biographical Notes on the Main Speakers

Air Chief Marshal Sir John Barraclough KCB CBE DFC AFC FRAeS FRSA

Commissioned in 1938, Sir John served in Coastal Command (Atlantic and North Sea) and the Middle East Air Force during the war. He took part in the Madagascar campaign and commanded the captured Italian airfield at Mogadishu. Later he commanded the RAF Fighter stations of Biggin Hill and Middleton St George and served in the Far East Air Force.

Sir John became Director of Public Relations for the RAF in 1961 and subsequent senior appointments were AOC No 19 Group, AOA Bomber/Strike Command, Vice Chief of Defence Staff, Air Secretary, and Commandant of the Royal College of Defence Studies, whence he retired in 1976.

In 1967 he took a sabbatical to attend the Harvard Business School Advanced Management Programme. Since retirement he has remained much involved with defence affairs being Chairman of the RUSI and Vice-Chairman of the Air League. He was Editorial Director of NATO's 15/16 NATIONS for several years and a co-author with General Sir John Hackett of THE THIRD WORLD WAR. Other appointments have included Vice-Chairman of the War Graves Commission and Hon. Inspector General of the Royal Auxiliary Air Force.

Mr John Terraine FRHistS

John Terraine was born in London in 1921 and educated at Stamford School and Keble College, Oxford. He joined the BBC in 1944 as a Recorded Programmes Assistant and did a variety of work including production of Radio Newsreel, programme assistant in the East European Service, and programme oganizer of the Pacific and South African service. In 1963 he became associate producer and scriptwriter of the BBC Television series 'The Great War', for which he received the Screenwriters' Guild Documentary Award. He left the BBC in 1964 and scripted 'The Life and Times of Lord Mountbatten' for Thames Television in 1966. In 1974 he was scriptwriter and narrator of the BBC series 'The Mighty Continent'.

He is the author of many books including ten titles about the First World War, and is also the founding President of the Western Front Association. His other books include a biography of Lord Mountbatten, The Mighty Continent and his most recent work, Business in Great Waters which is a study of the U-boat campaigns in both World Wars. In 1985 he wrote The Right of the Line, a major new study of the RAF's part in the Second World War, and now a standard text on the subject.

In 1982, to mark his contribution to military history, John Terraine received the Chesney Gold Medal, the highest award of the Royal United Services Institute for Defence Studies. In 1987 he became a Fellow of the Royal Historical Society.

Air Vice-Marshal W E Oulton CB CBE DSO DFC

Air Vice Marshal Wilf Oulton entered the RAF as a Flight Cadet at the RAF College Cranwell in 1929 and in 1932 joined 204 Squadron, equipped with Southampton flying boats. He later worked on the staff of the School of Air Navigation and in 1939 was flying Ansons with 217 Squadron. Later in the war, having served in the Air Ministry and on the British Air Staff in Washington, he flew Halifaxes and B17s in Coastal Command before taking command of the new base at Lagens, in the Azores, in 1943. Afterwards he commanded the flying boat base at Castle Archdale.

After the war he held a wide range of appointments, including command of the Task Force for the British H-bomb tests at Christmas Island, and before retiring at his own request in 1961 he spent 3 years as Chief of Staff at Northwood. He recently wrote an account of the Nuclear test operation, entitled 'Christmas Island Cracker'.

Lieutenant Commander WJR Gardener

Jock Gardner joined the Royal Navy in 1964, and has served in ships ranging from aircraft carriers to minesweepers. He is a specialist in anti-submarine warfare, and is currently serving in the Ministry of Defence in London. In 1989 he gained the degree of Master of Philosophy in International Relations at Cambridge University writing a thesis on the history and future of Soviet Ballistic-missile submarines. Whilst there he edited the Cambridge Review of International Affairs. Publications include articles on modern strategy in defence journals and historical papers, both in Britain and abroad. He has also contributed a short biography of Admiral Sir Bertram Ramsay to Men of War: Great Naval Leaders of World War Two edited by Stephen Howarth.

Mr Edward Thomas OBE

Edward Thomas studied German and music at University. He has had a long and varied career in Service and Defence Intelligence. During the Second World War he joined Naval Intelligence and served in Iceland, in the famous Hut 3 at Bletchley Park, and as Staff Officer (Intelligence) to the C-in-C Home Fleet in the Battleship DUKE OF YORK

His career continued in Strategic Intelligence after the war. A student of the Imperial Defence College, Mr Thomas has published translations of books by Helmut Schmidt and was co-author of the four-volume Official History of British Intelligence in the Second World War.

Dr Alfred Price PhD FRHistS

Alfred Price served in the Royal Air Force as an air electronics officer and, in a flying career spanning fifteen years, he specialized in electronic warfare.

In 1974 he left the RAF to become a full-time writer on aviation and related subjects. To date he has written 35 books and co-authored three more. Several of his books have become standard reference works on their respective subjects, including 'Instruments of Darkness' on the history of electronic warfare, 'The Hardest Day' on the Battle of Britain, 'Aircraft versus Submarine', on the history of airborne anti-submarine warfare, 'One Day in a Long War' on the air war over North Vietnam and 'Air War South Atlantic' on the Falklands conflict.

Professor Dr Jurgen Rohwer

Professor Rohwer served in the German Navy during World War II, engaged in minesweeping, and worked afterwards on similar duties under the Allied Control Commission. He then went to University and has since become one of Germany's leading authorities on the maritime war. His publications include 'Critical Convoy Battles of March 1943', 'Chronology of the War at Sea 1939-45', and 'Submarine Successes of the Maritime Powers 1939-45'. From 1959-1989 he was Curator of the Library of Contemporary History in Stuttgart.

Air Marshal Sir John Curtiss KCB KBE CBIM

Trained as a Navigator, Sir John Curtiss served first with Bomber Command on Halifaxes in the later stages of the war and then on Stirlings and Yorks in the transport role, including the Berlin Airlift. After a period in Fighter Control duties he served with 29 Squadron (Meteor night fighters) and 5 Squadron (Javelins), and then became Wing Commander Operations at Wittering, a Victor Medium Bomber station. He commanded Bruggen, a strike/attack Phantom station, spent some time at Headquarters Strike Command as Group Captain Operations, was SASO at 11 Group, and served at Bracknell as DS and later Commandant. He also served at MOD as Director General of Organization before becoming AOC 18 Group, the post he held at the time of the Falklands Conflict.

From 1985 to 1990 he was Director and Chief Executive of the Society of British Aerospace Companies.

Addendum

Comment on The Merchant Ship Fighter Unit
Submitted by Air Vice-Marshal M. Lyne

Since it was administered by Fighter Command MSFU's contribution to the Battle of the Atlantic could be easily overlooked. The main weight of attention will rightly be fixed on Coastal Command's sustained and ultimately successful battle against the submarine.

But it has to be remembered that in $2\frac{1}{2}$ months, from August 1940, the FW 200, Condor, an aircraft of roughly Lancaster proportions sank 90,000 tons of shipping. In late October a Condor even destroyed the 42,000 ton "Empress of Britain". These sinkings took place out of range of landbased fighters. The Navy had no carriers to spare for convoy protection and Coastal Command was not equipped to deal with these attacks.

There was anxious discussion of means of defence and the Navy started practical work with a catapult armed vessel carrying a rather slow Fulmar fighter. But the refined engineering needed for the naval catapult made it unsuitable for a rapid expansion and the arming of merchant ships. On 30th December, 1940 the decision was taken in principle to equip merchant ships to catapult fighters.

When the decision came firm and it was seen that an entirely new type of catapult would be needed, imaginative staff work led to the adoption of surplus rocket projectile motors, held in banks on the trolley and fired in succession, to power the launch. In consequence a "blacksmith's job" catapult was built and tested in about one month. It could accelerate a Hurricane to 70mph in one second (Porche eat your heart out).

Equipped now with Hurricanes the Navy drew first blood in July 1941, but in June the much more numerous RAF contribution had started. But it was not until May 1942 that the RAF had a combat. Then there was a double success on the Arctic route.

The absence of combats on the main Atlantic routes is a measure of the "Insurance Factor" provided by MSFU. This was boring for pilots, but good for the war effort. By the end of its life, around 30th July, 1943, MSFU ships had made 175 voyages. Of the 35 ships 12 had been lost to enemy action. One pilot was lost in action. A number of pilots and crews suffered exposure in open boats. Several were wounded in the air. One flew into the sea at high speed beating up his ship – and lived to tell the tale. One was reprimanded for flying down the main street at Halifax, Nova Scotia.

There were eight operational launches, one resulting in two enemy aircraft destroyed. The kill rate per sortie was over 0.8, probably the highest in the history of war over a long period.

The unit's inability to be "amenable to discipline" was shown at the end – formally disbanded by the Admiralty on 15 July 1943 it destroyed three Condors on 28th July.

One thing that made a profound impression on a young Flight Lieutenant as he watched the loading of general cargo in New York was the immense significance of the burden carried by the ungainly Empire Ships. Our cargo was said to be worth £3m. Our convoy home was of 110 ships, but lightly escorted by the Navy and Coastal Command.

Royal Air Force Historical Society

The Royal Air Force has been in existence for more than seventy years; the study of its history is deepening, and continues to be the subject of published works of consequence. Fresh attention is being given to the strategic assumptions under which military air power was first created and which largely determined policy and operations in both World Wars, the inter-war period, and in the era of Cold War tension. Material dealing with post-war history is now becoming available for study under the thirty-year rule. These studies are important both to academic historians and to the present and future members of the RAF.

The RAF Historical Society was formed in 1986 to provide a focus for interest in the history of the RAF. It does so by providing a setting for lectures and seminars in which those interested in the history of the RAF have the opportunity to meet those who participated in the evolution and implementation of policy. The Society believes that these events make an important contribution to the permanent record.

The Society normally holds three lectures or seminars a year in or near London, with occasional events in other parts of the country. Transcripts of lectures and seminars are published in the Proceedings of the RAF Historical Society, which is provided free of charge to members. Individual membership is open to all with an interest in RAF history, whether or not they were in the Service. Although the Society has the approval of the Air Force Board, it is entirely self-financing.

Membership of the Society costs £15 per annum and further details may be obtained from the Membership Secretary, Commander Peter Montgomery, 26 Shirley Drive, Worthing, West Sussex BN14 9AY.

Shell U.K. Oil

*The Royal Air Force Historical Society
wishes to record
grateful and sincere thanks
to Shell Aviation
for its generous help.*